WAS THAT A SIGN FROM HEAVEN?

How to connect with the *Afterlife*

LISA WILLIAMS

Animal Dreaming Publishing
www.AnimalDreamingPublishing.com

Was that a Sign from Heaven?
How to connect with the Afterlife

ANIMAL DREAMING PUBLISHING
PO Box 5203 East Lismore NSW 2480
AUSTRALIA
Phone +61 2 6622 6147
www.AnimalDreamingPublishing.com
www.facebook.com/AnimalDreamingPublishing
Email: publish@animaldreamingpublishing.com

Originally published in 2014 by 'LWISSD Publications' under the title
'I Speak to Dead People. Can you?'
'Was that a Sign from Heaven? How to connect with the Afterlife'
has been revised, reformatted and redesigned.

First published 2016
Copyright text © 2016 Lisa Williams

Cover Copyright © Animal Dreaming Pubishing
Design and Layout Copyright © Animal Dreaming Publishing

ISBN: 978-0-9953642-0-2

The information in this book is intended for spiritual and emotional guidance
only. It is not intended to replace medical advice or treatment.

Designed by Animal Dreaming Publishing
Printed in the USA

This book is dedicated to Shirley Millin, my first student.
Without you I wouldn't be sharing the teachings and messages,
and creating the ripple effect around the world.
You are always in my heart.

CONTENTS

ACKNOWLEDGMENTS

Charlie, for the light that you are in my world. My parents, for your continual love and support. Karen Fritschi, for keeping me going through all the good times and bad. David, Ryan, Chris, Scott and Donna for being the inspiration and motivation in many areas of my world. To my friends Laurie, Sarah, Janey, Janice, Denise, Colette, Liz, Jo, Angelique and Harry T. All of you have kept me believing in my journey, and you have all inspired me in your own way and have given me faith. I love you all.

WAS THAT A SIGN FROM HEAVEN?

HOW TO CONNECT WITH THE AFTERLIFE.

Thank you for joining me on this journey and I am honored that you trust me to help you you're your connection to your loved ones further. Throughout this journey, you will have a great deal of fun, but it will take dedication.

This book is designed for those who wish to develop their natural gifts or to understand more about the afterlife and see the signs that their loved ones are around them.

Firstly, let me introduce myself. My name is Lisa Williams, and I have been working as a psychic medium for over twenty years. I never planned to work as a medium. I mean, think about it: in the '80s, having a career as a medium was never heard of. If I had gone to my teachers and said, "I want to speak to dead people for a career," I would have been carted off to the nearest mental institute. In fact, there were times that my mother would joke about the men in white coats coming to get me. I thought she was serious, and I grew up thinking that I was a little weird and hiding my ability.

I was lucky to have a friend who thought my weirdness was cool. She was always asking questions about it, so I started to feel more comfortable; but as friends do, we drifted apart, and I had a new circle of friends, so I went back into the closet. I still had a growing intuition, but I curbed it and didn't say anything. I just found that I "knew" things, and I couldn't really explain it. I was actually quite shy growing up, and I found that I conformed with society about what I believed I should be like. It was easy. I fit the mold, and I didn't say anything...many people would call that being a sheep and following the crowd.

Does this sound familiar to your story? It probably does.

Well let me tell you: you are normal. Just because you have this gift doesn't mean that you have to hide it. For years I hid from it. I even hid it from my own parents for a while. For most of my life, my father has been a huge skeptic, and I remember the time when I had been working as a psychic medium for a while and he asked me when I was going to get a "proper job." He was an atheist and couldn't wrap his head around the concept that our soul continues to live on when our body dies.

When I finally decided to come out as a medium, it was accepted and most people had a fascination about it. It was "cool" to have this gift. I grew up in the United Kingdom and so we never showed emotions, never went to therapy, and we never said we loved each other. It was a very different world to what we live in now. Going to a psychic or a medium was better than going to a therapist in the United Kingdom. When you went to the therapist you were admitting that you had a problem, it was a sign of weakness. Now it's considered a gift to be aware of your challenges, and it's actually character building.

I finally surrendered to my gift after my friend helped me see that I wasn't crazy and that I actually could help others. The rest is history.

What I would have benefited from, though, in those early years was some structure, discipline, and understanding.

Even though my grandmother worked as a medium she died before I started, and so I didn't have anyone really to talk too. The only thing that she said to me was:

"Always trust your gut instincts. It will never let you down."

That is something I live by, and I will suggest that you do, too.

Through my work, I have been guided by Spirit, which has shown me the way forward to work with my gift. I have built my gift on discipline and respect, which is something that I will enforce within you. I have developed the skill of delivering a message, as well as enhancing and fine-tuning my gift. These are things that I will help you with.

Throughout this book you will come to understand the history of Mediumship, how to develop your gift, and how to see signs from your loved ones. You will be given daily exercises to enhance your gift and to help you connect to your own loved ones and those of other people.

Each week we will cover a different topic that you will have to commit to for at least half an hour daily. I have written this by days so that it's easy for you to keep track. I suggest that each night you read the next day so that you are prepared. There are some days that you will have to do an exercise all day, so knowing the day before is important. If you have to miss a day, then that's OK; I certainly don't want you to be stressed, but read the work, and then do what you feel is needed. Always listen to your instincts, and you will be guided internally.

Before you start, there are some things that you need to prepare.

You need to explain to your friends and family that you are studying mediumship, and you won't be as available as you have been previously.

- You need a space to work, somewhere quiet so that you can meditate.
- You may need headphones or earplugs if you don't have a peaceful home.
- You will need friends and family to help you.
- You will need a journal and a pen that are strictly for this work.

It is all right to work in groups. Sometimes friends all work together and help each other stay focused.

WELCOME TO WEEK *One*

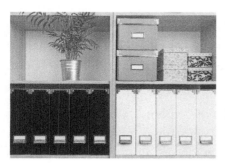

This is an exciting time as you embark on your journey with Spirit. You may have been experiencing some signs or you may be working as a medium and wanting to go back to basics to enhance your gift. Whatever the reason that is personal to you.

This week we will be focusing on you as a person. Personally I love this week, as we will be decluttering the environments around you. I often find that when we are organized and we have space in our life, we have space for Spirit and Spirituality. When we take pride in who we are, then we have pride in everything that we do. This is important to maintain in every aspect of our life.

You may find that you are already an organized person and if that is the case then I would still urge you to continue with the week, but focus on some environments that need it. If you already have pride in everything that you do, then be mindful of this and no longer are you going through the motions with life, consciously think about everything that you do and say.

It's an enlightening week and no matter who you are you will always get what you need. Enjoy!

Day 1

Over the duration of this book, you will be setting boundaries and becoming free from restrictions. To work with Spirit, or even just connect with your loved ones, you need to make space, and you need to allow and accept Spirit into your life. It's not as easy as many people believe, but with a little trust and belief you can accomplish many things.

Firstly, let me explain why I talk of "Spirit." Well, to me Spirit are a collective energies of souls who have crossed over to the afterlife. Spirit can represent one person or many, each individual's perception is different. Some people also include Spirit Guides as part of that energy. We will discuss Spirit Guides in a few weeks, however, if you have already established a connection to your guide, then this is wonderful, and I strongly urge you to keep that connection open.

I must also state here, in order for you not to be confused, that I will refer to you and your living Spirit as the 'soul'—the true essence of who you are. Your soul is the energy that eventually transitions over to the afterlife. After the transition, it becomes Spirit. This saves any confusion as to whether the "being" that I am talking about is physically alive on this earth plane or not.

Essentially, both are the same thing; one is on the earth plane while the other is in the afterlife.

While you are opening yourself to the world of Spirit, you also have to open yourself up to your own soul and love yourself. You will have to do this over the next two months, and once it becomes a habit, you will find that it will become part of your daily practice, and it will change your life in many ways.

You are coming on this journey to connect with Spirit for a reason. Whatever your reason is, it is a personal thing that you must honor. The reason will change and evolve over the next few months. By the end, you may wish to work with Spirit more or you may wish to walk away. Whatever you decide is right for you. There is no right and wrong with Spirit; they will honor your decisions, whatever they may be. Remember that spirits have lived a life on this earth plane, so they know the decisions and the choices that we have to make. You will never be judged for what you decide to do in your world. Just know that you are loved and appreciated for who you are.

Today's Exercise

You are now going to go within yourself and examine why you are reading this. Why do you wish to connect with Spirit? Before you do so, there are some things that I would like you to do.

Find a space that is quiet, where you can relax and will not be disturbed.

Get your journal and pen. You may also wish to have some water.

Ensure that you are sitting comfortably and that you are not lying down.

If you wish, put on some relaxing music softly in the background. It is best to avoid music that is going to stimulate your mind or trigger any memories. I suggest some soft meditation music.

Now that you are sitting quietly, you are going to focus on your breath. Count the breaths you take in and out for two minutes. Breath is the sacred energy of the universe that keeps us alive. By focusing on your breath, you remove any thoughts or emotions you are currently holding. If thoughts do enter your mind, just allow yourself to come back to focus on counting your breaths. Allow your breath to be easy and natural.

Sit in a comfortable space and count the breaths you take in and out of your body for two minutes. This will help you relax and free your mind from thoughts. If thoughts do enter your mind, just allow yourself to come back to focus on counting your breaths.

With your journal ready, you need to ask yourself the following questions:

• Why am I on this journey of connecting with Spirit?

• What do I want to achieve by studying mediumship?

Allow yourself about fifteen to twenty minutes to get your answers and write everything. You may believe that you know the answer before you start this exercise, but you may be surprised by what comes to you.

Just allow the information to flow. No one will judge you; just appreciate what you have been given.

Now that you have been given this, it's time to reflect on what you are going to do. Dedicate this moment to you and remember this moment as being sacred. It could be the first step toward changing your life.

Day 2

Yesterday, you started your journey and examined the reasons why you are here. It's now time to fully commit and create a space for you to work with Spirit.

Today you are going to start to create your boundaries. This work is something that you have to dedicate yourself to in order to get the best results. Although you are a spiritual being, you will still need to live a human existence. This human experience is going to be essential for your own personal growth in a spiritual sense.

Let me explain. The reason why I believe I have gotten so far with my work as a medium is because I have experienced so much. I have had no home, suffered major health issues, almost lost my life, and many other things along the way. I certainly do not want any sympathy because, quite honestly, I wouldn't be able to connect with people in the way that I do without these experiences. They have helped me understand what others go through and therefore have increased the value of my gift.

To be a medium you will have to experience many things: heartaches, upsets, love, and laughter. Just about every emotion you can imagine, you will have to go through. And the reason?

To appreciate what others go through and to help them on their journeys

Locking yourself away in a closet is no good for anyone. You need to step out and be proud of who you are. Live your life and appreciate all that you have and are given. Good and bad.

Within the human life, you need to make room for Spirit; therefore, you are going to create a space for your work.

Today's Exercise

Choose a place in your home that you can work in—a place that is peaceful or relaxing that you know you can dedicate to Spirit. I know what it's like in a busy household. I'm a mother. You may have to choose your bathroom so you can lock the door and shut away the rest of the family. You may choose the living room, kitchen, or even bathroom as I have suggested, but if possible keep your bedroom free from this work. You do not want to connect to Spirit in a place that you sleep unless you are experienced enough to push them away so that you can have a good night's sleep. Your sleep is vital, so keep your bedroom as a safe haven.

Sit and examine the space that you have chosen to be your Spirit place for about five minutes. Sit and look at everything. Close your eyes and connect with your breath as you did before and then ask yourself the following questions:

Is the space—which includes the whole room—cluttered and untidy?

1. Are the corners cluttered and stuffed with items?
2. Do you have a lot of raw crystals grouped together?
3. Are the curtains in the space closed?
4. Are the windows constantly kept shut?
5. Does the energy feel stagnant or "stuck?"
6. Are you uncomfortable in this space?
7. Are you finding it hard to relax here?

If answered yes to three or more questions, then you need to change what is in this space. You need to create a place of tranquility. Often when we have clutter in the room that we choose to work in, it is also mirrored in our lives. We have clutter and drama in our lives. It's time to clear it out. Take time to make this place a haven for your spiritual growth.

Declutter the room. Throw away or donate unwanted items. If you don't want them, don't keep them "just because." Let them go. If they are items from loved ones who have passed and you are holding on to them for them, decide if you like the items first. If you don't like them, surely your loved ones would want you to share the items with people who would appreciate them. Reposition items, if you need too.

Make sure all the corners of the room are free and not cluttered. Energy tends to be attracted to corners and get stuck, so having free corners will help the energy flow around the room.

If you have lots of raw crystals gathered together, then it's time to find a new home for them. Small, smooth tumbled stones are fine together, but raw crystals emit a great deal of energy. When you have lots of energy gathered in one space, it can work against itself and result in conflict, so space the raw crystals out. The size of the raw crystals will determine the space needed between them. If they are small raw crystals that fit in the palm of your hand, then they can be about a foot apart, however, if they are bigger, give them their own space. These are beautiful pieces. Allow them their own space.

The windows and curtains need to open, and you need to allow fresh energy to come into the space. Opening the windows will help the energy flow and disperse any energy buildup.

When you change these things, you will find that the energy will no longer be stagnant, and you will start to feel comfortable in the space. Create this space and keep it clear. Choose calming colors and try to stick to one or two accent colors in the room so that it's not overpowering.

Place things in this space that you want. Things that inspire you, photos, candles, and items that are important to you.

By doing this, you will feel so much better. It may cause you to go through the rest of the house, and that's OK. It's essential for you to create this space now.

This room will be your space for the next two months while you work on your connection to your loved ones. It needs to be welcoming and warm to those who enter, and this includes Spirit.

Please be aware that when you start to declutter your home, you will find that you start to declutter your life, and therefore people who have been part of your world may leave. And that is OK; they are no longer serving you. When you work with Spirit, you will start to understand things in a much larger scale, and while it's hard sometimes to let people go, it's for your own spiritual growth. You may choose to let go of some while others will leave because you are no longer serving them, which means they are no longer serving you.

Once you have decluttered and created the room in the way that you wish, spend fifteen minutes just sitting in this space. Experience how you feel in this place.

If you get any thoughts or feelings, write them down in your journal.

Unless you are guided otherwise, you are now going to work in this space.

Day 3

As I have said, Spirit never judge and they appreciate every aspect of you. The father who judged you, the mother who was bitter, the sister who was jealous, the friends or lovers who didn't appreciate what you gave them... after crossing all of these souls will not judge you or have these feelings toward you anymore. The afterlife is a place of beauty and love, and all of these earthly feelings will be released. Whether you wish to believe it or not, they have. I wrote about it in my book *Survival of the Soul*. The Spirit releases all the negativity and surrenders to a place of love. It's quite remarkable.

Now is the time to appreciate you. You need to see the beauty within yourself. Know that you can help yourself and you can help others.

One thing that I talk a great deal about is *trust*, and you will not be able to succeed with the communication without trusting the information that you are given.

Let me put this to you. Many people trust the information that I give them when I give a psychic or a mediumistic reading. They trust me because I have a reputation, and they believe that I am giving them messages directly from Spirit. While this is correct, they also trust me because I haven't let them down. That's the reality. If you are let down by someone, you are less likely to trust them. The more and more you are let down by them, the more the trust will leave, and you will lose your faith in that person. It's very similar to the work with Spirit.

If I gave a reading and every piece of evidence and information was incorrect, then you would not trust me to do a reading for you again. However, the one person that you can and should trust is *yourself*. But you don't. Throughout life you have been told that you are not good enough and that you can't be trusted. You have let yourself down so many times; for instance, you have said that you are going to exercise, and then you suddenly stop, and you beat yourself up. You are your own worst enemy. Well, it's time to *stop* this thought pattern.

You *have* to start to have faith and trust in yourself. If you don't, then you will not believe what you are getting from Spirit. You will not trust the signs that you get from your loved ones. You will question everything that you get. So this has to *stop* now!

Today's Exercise

You need to fully appreciate yourself.

Today you are going to honor who you are!

- Every time you look in the mirror, you are going to smile at yourself.

- Every time you catch yourself saying something negative toward yourself, you are going to stop and appreciate who you are.

- When you get dressed, you are going to take pride in your appearance and dress for you!

- You are going to fully appreciate who you are: the loving and caring soul that you are, who many people appreciate and see.

You are also going to contact five people you know and ask each of them to give you five words that describe the person you are. This can be interesting especially if you ask a mixture of people including work colleagues, friends, and family.

This is how people see you. You have to stop being so hard on yourself, and you have to see the beauty that others see. This is part of your spiritual growth.

You are going to write those words in your journal at the end of the day, and then you are going to write a letter to yourself about how much you appreciate yourself and what you like and admire about who you are. Allow the words to flow through you. You can ask for guidance from the afterlife if you wish.

Next you are going to place this letter in the sacred space that you created. Allow the letter to be a constant reminder of who you are.

You are going to continue this practice of honoring who you are throughout the remainder of this book. Every time you have self-doubt, you will reverse it into positivity.

YOU ARE BEAUTIFUL, COURAGEOUS, AND INSPIRING.

Day 4

Today is a day of boundaries. You may not like this but, as part of your connection to Spirit, you need to release your "escapes" in life. The things that you do to escape life, such as social media, reading novels, watching TV shows and movies, checking e-mails, online shopping…just about anything you use to hide from the world.

In my advanced courses, I make the students give up *everything* for the duration of their course. They find that with the simple life comes the simple things that matter, and they create boundaries. This is essential in life. I'm not going to do this with you, but I am going to ask you to set boundaries.

Let me explain. When you are a sensitive being, you will find that people will constantly want from you, and they will take everything that you are prepared to give. Sometimes you have to learn to say no and to stand strong with your views. There is nothing wrong with this, and if you create your boundaries now, then they will be respected.

You need to create boundaries with:

- yourself
- friends
- family
- Spirit

So now it's time to think about people and situations that drain you, tire you, and then create boundaries. We live in a world where people "expect" us to be constantly "available." We have e-mails, social media outlets, and Internet on our phones with "push alerts" so that every time someone contacts us, we are notified. We have text messages. People would rather have a text conversation than pick up the phone. We feel the need to share our lives with everyone on social media. Are they really interested in your dinner and what it looks like? People "check in" and share where they are; you are "poked" by strangers; and you have so-called "friends," many of whom you don't have an association with and maybe haven't for years.

We are constantly available and in touch, and we have lost the connection to what is real. That is you, your family, and friends.

People expect you to respond to them, through text messages, e-mails, and other means. What happened to being home and relaxing? We aren't. As you go about your day, notice how many people are on their phones while they stand in line for coffee or are at the store. Look around at those in restaurants and the couples and groups that are all on their phones.

It's time to be present.

Today's Exercise

Set yourself a boundary. If you have social media apps on your phone, remove them, and only go on the sites when you are on the actual computer. Turn off the computer at least an hour before you go to bed. Connect with family and friends via verbal communication, such as picking up the phone and talking to them or meeting them for lunch rather than having a text conversation.

You have the right to have a life, which means your phone doesn't have to be attached to you. The world will still revolve while you are not connected.

Don't escape in a book all the time. Set aside an hour a day for reading then put it down and spend time with your family, friends, and Spirit.

Say to Spirit that you will only connect with them when you give them the signal. Create a signal. Mine is my watch. If I have my watch on or any metal around my wrist then that means I am off duty, but when it's removed, they can come along and have a chat with me. Set a signal and tell them. For instance, if you always wear a certain ring, then tell them that whenever you take it off you are free to communicate with them. Trust me, as much as you want this you will also have to set boundaries. You can't always be connected.

Your friends and family, if they appreciate who you are, will respect your need for space over this period of time while you are studying. If they ask you to do something and you don't want too, or you don't feel like it, then don't do it. Say no…

you have the right to do that, and if they don't like it, that's their problem. You are not to feel guilty. Remember who you are. Go back to the letter you wrote to yourself.

Setting boundaries is essential in life. Otherwise we would have no time for anything.

So today start to create boundaries with social media, e-mails, text messages, and also friends and family. Take time to honor yourself.

Continue this as you go through your learning, and you will appreciate the space that you are creating in your life.

Day 5

Today you are going to connect with Spirit. At the moment, you are not going to connect with one of your loved ones; you are going to work with a Spirit whom I know well and will work with you.

Spirit will want to work with you.

I must, at this time, explain the difference between being a psychic and a medium. A psychic can connect to your life and the life path. Mediums are also psychic, but they connect directly to Spirit. Now there are many psychics who will say that they are connecting with your loved ones, but they are not. You will be thinking about your loved one and a situation or a memory that you both shared, and suddenly the psychic will connect to that memory and your loved one. Immediately you, as the client, will think that the psychic is connecting to Spirit when in fact the psychic is not. What the psychic is doing is connecting to the information that you are transmitting through your energy. That's what psychics do: they read energy and your life path. This is an amazing gift, and its one I love working with, but I always tell my clients when I am working psychically and mediumistically.

Today's Exercise

While you may think that this is a psychic exercise, it's actually a good exercise in believing and trusting what you get. Whether you feel the Spirit, just know information, or you connect on a psychic level and you doubt that you are connecting to Spirit; I want you to *trust* and give everything that you are getting.

Sit in your sacred space and breathe. Focus on your breath and know that you are just being present in your life. When you are ready, I would like you to turn to the photo of the Spirit at the end of this section and answer the following questions.

1. What is this person's name or what initial does his name start with?

2. What is this person's relationship to myself?

3. What is this person's personality?

4. What are his likes and dislikes?

5. How many children does this person have?

6. Do you know what sex the children are?

7. How did this person pass?

8. What was this person's career?

9. What is one significant memory or situation that we shared?

10. What nationality is this person?

Don't fear being wrong…just *believe*. Trust me, he will work with you. All you have to do is ask!

Write down your answers, and when you have finished, say thank you to the Spirit, open your windows, and walk away from your work. Go and do something normal, such as cooking, gardening, or hanging out with friends.

Well done. This is a huge lesson of trust!

The answers for the questions are at the back of the book.

Day 6

You have had six days of being present, and you should be exceptionally proud of yourself. It's hard to create boundaries and keep them, but as you go through this book you will find it gets easier. You have created your space and set these boundaries, which are essential for your spiritual growth. Now the next step in your growth is connecting with yourself and who you are through meditation.

Meditation is essential for any spiritual growth, however, I will put a myth to bed: you don't need to meditate to connect with Spirit. We open up...which some would call meditation. But meditation is essentially you connecting with yourself and your own soul. Once you connect with your own soul, you will find that it's easier to connect to other souls, whether they are here or passed.

Have you ever noticed that when you relax and do something easy and routine that you can feel Spirit around you? Have you noticed that when the phone rings you know who it is or that you think of people and next thing you receive messages from them? This is because you are connecting with your soul and your soul connects to others. I like to think of it as the underground network of souls. Every soul is connected to another, one way or another.

Meditation will help you connect.

You may think that you can't meditate because you are unable to totally clear your mind of any thoughts or feelings. If you can clear your mind then that is wonderful, but most people won't be able to initially. I will teach you focus in a few weeks, but first let's start with simple breath work, which is the basis of any meditation.

You have already been doing this without realizing by just focusing on your breath and counting how many breaths come in and out of your body over the space of two minutes.

Meditation will also allow you to be a clear channel for Spirit. You hear yourself and Spirit when you meditate. Meditating is just being focused and present.

Many people think that you have to sit in the lotus position or stare at a candle; reality is that as you can meditate many ways. Sometimes when I am running on the treadmill I zone out and get so many messages and inspiration. I can walk my dogs and get the same messages or sit at the piano. There are many ways to get into that space.

Today's Exercise

We are now going to start a meditation practice. You will do daily meditation, which is going to be essential to your work on connecting to Spirit.

Set a timer for two minutes with a gentle, easy alarm, and then focus on your breathing, counting the breaths that come in and out of your body.

Allow your body to relax with each breath that you take into your body. When the alarm goes off, stay in that position and allow your mind to stay focused. When thoughts and feelings come in, allow them to come in and then wash away. You are then going to connect to your soul and feel how you are feeling.

What are your feelings at the moment toward the work you are doing? Are you happy? Is there anything that you would like to change? Use your journal to write everything that you get…. Allow the pen to glide over the page and write whatever comes to you. Don't process or think about what you are writing. You are connecting with your soul and possibly Spirit. We will call this your 'Connection Meditation'.

You can read the information that you are given after you receive it.

Enjoy this experience and make it your daily practice for the next week. You will find it will help you connect to Spirit.

Congratulations on completing the first week. It may seem like a lot of information, but I can tell you that it's essential for your growth and connection to Spirit. It's part of being disciplined and having respect for Spirit. Remember that Spirit does not judge. They love you for who you are, so enjoy every experience that you have with them.

Day 7—Review Day

Every week you will have a day to review your week and your work with Spirit. Please answer the following questions in your journal.

1. What do you want to achieve by studying mediumship?
2. Did you have to spend much time decluttering a space for your work?
3. How did you honor yourself on Day 3? What did you find you changed about how you view yourself?
4. Did you find it difficult to create boundaries?
5. How was your connection to the Spirit in the photograph on Day Five? Did you find it easy or hard?
6. How was your first day of meditating and writing in your journal?

WELCOME TO WEEK *Two*

O ften the first week is the hardest since you are setting boundaries and making goals and plans. You are motivated to start something, and you are excited. You just need to keep that motivation within you and continue your growth. Because it is growth as much as discovering the opportunities that the afterlife presents, and living in the present, and knowing that you have been put onto this earth plane for a reason. Actually, you chose your pathway before you came to the earth plane as a baby.

Situations may have changed in your home because, when you change the energy, you will find that you start to change everything about your life, as your home is the root to you. When you physically make changes, you will emotionally make changes, no matter how subtle they are. And with this you have probably noticed how some people *really* irritate you and others just get on your nerves. What is interesting is that, when you analyze it, you will find it's the people that you least expect who drive you a little mad.

This is very normal in the mediumistic world.

This week we are going to look at the history of spiritualism and the masters of spiritualism. We are also going to look at energy, what it is, and where it is. So get ready for an action packed and fun week.

Day 8
History of Spiritualism

I personally believe that you should know a little about the history of where this started and how it became as popular as it is today. It's like anything: we have to have some appreciation of the background. Especially during the beginning stages of development since then you have the knowledge and can go into the gift with a full understanding of those who have surrendered their lives for this.

Spiritualism is the correct title for the discipline that includes Mediumship. Mediumship is being the middleman that bridges the gap from this world to the next. Allan Kardec was instrumental in the phenomenon of Mediumship. He became fascinated in the subject and went to many mediums to ask about Mediumship and the meaning of life. He called it Spiritism, so if you ever research the subject, you may come across his name. I won't make you read his books for this, as they are extremely hard to read since they have been translated from French, however, they are fascinating to me. When I read his book *The Spirit Book*, I found that much of the information that I had been "told" from Spirit for my book *Survival of the Soul* was in fact the same as his book. I just believe that mine is a little easier to read.

The modern-day movement in spiritualism started in 1848 with three sisters: Margaret, Kate, and Leah Fox. However, communicating with deceased loved ones, channeling Spirits, trance work, and healing have been around for thousands of years. The ancient Greeks used to channel the oracles and go into trances, often speaking in different voices and expressing personalities different than their own. It is documented how the Earth's natural elements, such as crystals, have healing properties and were the only source of medication at one point, and it's a method that is still used today. Even in the Bible, Mediumship is documented. So we are extremely naive to think that Mediumship has only been around for a few hundred years.

However, the modern-day movement of spiritualism started in 1848, the reason being that this was the first time that it was documented. What happened actually was a big deal, and it expanded all over the world.

It was in 1848 that the Fox sisters, who lived in Hydesville, New York, started to spread the word of Mediumship and the connection that they had to the Spirit World.

The Fox family moved into their home on December 11, 1847, and from that day they heard noises in the house—noises that were more than creaking floorboards and animals moving outside. These were strange echoes and rappings that were physically heard. After searching the home for all the obvious reasons for these noises, they found nothing.

It was on March 31, 1848, when Margaret and Kate (the younger sisters) had just gone to bed, that the rappings started again. The intrigued children started to communicate with the Spirit of a murdered peddler. They set up a code of rappings. The Spirit communicated with raps to answer questions that the girls asked. This is how the sisters determined whom they were talking to. The family gathered the neighbors to witness this phenomenon. Therefore this is the first documented record of Mediumship. The Spirit gave his audience specific details about how he was murdered, and the amazed neighbors continued to communicate with the Spirit even when Mrs. Fox took her daughters out of the house for the night.

The following night, their home was the source of entertainment with people gathering from all around to experience the phenomenon that today we know as Physical Mediumship.

The story of the Fox sisters is actually really interesting since they continued to work as mediums under the management of their older sister, Leah. Of course everyone wanted to prove that it was not real. The Fox sisters gained quite a following and were successful within the Spiritualist movement. However, after a bitter argument with Leah and other Spiritualists in 1888, Margaret confessed to the press and admitted that Mediumship was a fraudulent act. This was for financial gain; she had been offered $1500 to admit it was a lie. Margaret and Kate had become heavy drinkers, and this was the source of the argument with Leah. They had gotten themselves into financial difficulty, and so the false confession was Margaret's way of gaining some money. She said that the noises that the apparent Spirit had made were sounds she made when cracking the bones in her feet. She created the sound. However, that statement was retracted a year later. None of them worked as successful mediums after that, and each sister passed away within five years of this incident.

It wasn't until 1904 that a skeleton was discovered underneath the home where the Fox sisters lived when they first heard the rappings.

This physical phenomenon reached England in 1852 by way of a Boston medium, Mrs. Hayden. Many started to explore it, and I believe that it was bigger, and probably still is, in England than it is elsewhere in the world.

Over the 150-plus years since the first recorded event by Margaret and Kate Fox there has been a vast array of phenomena produced by the Spirit World.

One of the most famous Physical Mediums was a woman called Helen Duncan, a Scottish housewife who traveled throughout the United Kingdom during World War II holding séances, providing communication from this world to the next. One of her séances was raided by a plain-clothes police officer who blew his whistle and tried to grab the ectoplasm, claiming that it was a white sheet. The ectoplasm pulled back into the body of the medium extremely quickly, so there was nothing that he could grab.

Ectoplasm is a physical matter that looks like a 'cheesecloth' that comes from the orifices of a physical medium. The Spirit creates this appearance by using the energy that is shared by the medium and moisture in the air. The physical eye in light conditions will not see it and a dark room is needed.

Because of Helen's practices she was imprisoned under the 1735 Witchcraft Act. Sir Winston Churchill used to visit her and told her that he would make amends. She served her time and was released in September 1944. The Prime Minister served the Spiritual movement well, and he replaced the Witchcraft Act with the Fraudulent Mediums Act and in 1954 a formal Act of Parliament officially recognized spiritualism as a religion.

However, this didn't stop skeptics, and as Helen was holding another séance the police raided it. This time the police did the unthinkable to a medium holding a demonstration and grabbed the medium. This can cause fatal damage. The ectoplasm withdrew quickly into Helen's body leaving second degree burns across her stomach, and she became extremely ill and died five weeks later.

It's a sad story, but Helen Duncan was brave, courageous, and owned her gift, surrendering her life to Spirit and providing evidence that life continues on. She never wavered and was proud to do the work that she was placed on this earth to do. She changed the way that people approach spiritualism, certainly within the United Kingdom.

For me it's a remarkable story and a fascinating one. She paved the way for many, including myself, who continue in her pathway, surrendering to Spirit and opening the doors for communication to the afterlife.

But it's the story of the Fox sisters that actually proves my point: that you can be an amazing medium *but* not necessarily a spiritual person, so spirituality and spiritualism do not always go hand in hand.

Religion and Spiritualism

While people are entitled to their own beliefs, I think it's important to address religion here. Some would say that spiritualism is a religion, however, it actually isn't, yet with the title of the Spiritual Church it is often categorized in that field.

I had a situation many years ago that taught me a huge lesson about spirituality and religion The Jehovah's Witness who was standing at my door said, "If I hadn't been brought up in the Jehovah's Witness faith, then I may believe in what you believe in. However, as long as you have a belief, that's all that matters as it leads you to have a belief in yourself, and that is ultimately what we are striving for." It showed me that religion and spirituality *can* and *do* work hand in hand.

Here are some quotes from the Bible to think about:

"But the fruit of the Spirit is love, joy, peace, patience, kindness, goodness, faithfulness," —Galatians 5:22

"The mind governed by the flesh is death, but the mind governed by the Spirit is life and peace." —Romans 8:6

"Dear friends, do not believe every spirit, but test the spirits to see whether they are from God, because many false prophets have gone out into the world." —1 John 4:1

Today's Exercise

Think about your own beliefs. You will experience many people who have different opinions about this work, but it's *you* who have to decide what you are going to do and how you are going to be in your life. Remember this is *your* life, and no one has the right to tell you what to do or how to be. We have been "conditioned" in life to think a certain way. So now it's time for you to just accept you. Don't let anyone tell you any different.

For the rest of the day, think about how you are going to share your beliefs with other people. You may wish to go into your sacred space and write out a statement of your beliefs so that you can live your life by those daily and not be afraid to share them with anyone who asks.

Go to your sacred space and do your Connection w. Concentrate on your breath for two minutes, and then sit in a state of peace and just allow thoughts and feelings to come and go, and write anything that you feel is profound in your journal. Remember this is something you will continue daily for the next week.

Days 9 and 10

Now that you have the knowledge and understanding of the history of Mediumship, it is time for research. YouTube has become something that people watch more than TV, and we can find so many fascinating and wondrous topics to view on here. So over this book you will find that you will refer to it a great deal.

As I have said, it's important for you to know who has paved the pathway for Mediumship in the past, but now we need to bring our attention into the present.

When we think of Spiritual masters, we often think of Gandhi, Buddha, the Dalai Lama, Deepak Chopra, Wayne Dyer, and many others. People follow them since their teachings have shown us the light and have taught us to be the spiritual beings that we are. While these souls certainly should not be disregarded, within the spiritualism world there are many others that are not the recognized names that many know. These masters have opened the door that has paved the way forward for many future mediums. We need to explore them and give them the credit that they so dutifully deserve.

Past Masters

Allan Kardec

Edgar Cayce

Margaret and Kate Fox

Helen Duncan

Doris Stokes

Arthur Findlay

Sylvia Browne

Present Masters

John Edward

James Van Praagh

Tony Stockwell

Past Masters

Allan Kardec

Hippolyte Léon Denizard Rivali was born in Lyons in 1804 to a family of distinguished lawyers and magistrates. He was born in a Catholic society but raised a Christian and spent many hours thinking about the religious beliefs and questioned everything, proving that he was very much a free thinker.

He also had a passion for teaching and after completing his schooling he was to return home and follow the family tradition of law but found himself teaching Chemistry, Physics, Comparative Anatomy and Astronomy and made a name for himself in this field publishing various highly esteems articles.

It was around 1850 when the phenomenon of 'table tipping' started that Rivali became interested in Spirits. An associate of his had two daughters who were mediums and his fascination grew, and over a two year period asked the mediums while they were under trance communication to the Spirit world questions about life and death.

He had gained a great deal of knowledge about the afterlife and asked Spirit the question about what he should do with it.

"To the book in which you will embody our instructions, you will give, as being our work rather than yours, the title of *Le Livre des Espirts (The Spirits' Book)* and you will publish it, not under your own name, but under the *pseudonym* of ALLAN KARDEC."

On April 18, 1857, Allan Kardec published his first book on Spiritism, *The Spirits' Book*, which contains the questions and answers that he received from his Spirit communications.

This book was translated into English in 1881. He continued to write books that are an incredible source of knowledge for those who are interested in the Spirit World

Edgar Cayce

Edgar Cayce is probably one of the most documented psychics in of the 20th Century. He was born in Kentucky in 1877 and like many displayed psychic abilities in his childhood and spoke to his grandfathers' spirit and had many 'imaginary friends'. He was known as the 'sleeping prophet' and the 'father of holistic medicine' as he gave his readings while lying down with his eyes closed in a sleeping position. He would answer many questions regarding past lives, and lives that were yet to come and also diagnosing illnesses. His readings were incredibly accurate and extremely helpful to those who needed guidance and healing.

What was interesting is that he was a devoted churchgoer and also Sunday school teacher. His aim as to bring religion and spirituality together and when asked how to be psychic his response was to be more spiritual, and he is correct that is what is needed to develop this gift.

He focused at being one with himself, which is something that we embrace now but many years ago, it was never really heard of and he bought a spiritual approach to his work.

Her certainly paved the way for many psychic mediums and his readings are still extremely relevant to many people today as they talk about various topics such as spiritual growth, auras, meditation and so much more. You can access the entire set of 14,306 readings in the database at the Edgar Cayce's Association for Research and Enlightenment (A.R.E.)

Margaret and Kate Fox

We explored the two sisters last lesson. Their lives were incredible and opened the door for modern day spiritualism. Even though they didn't honor their gift in the end and suggested that they were frauds for monetary gain, they certainly brought spiritualism to the forefront in many ways. It became the phenomenon it is today because of the rapping that they heard from the murdered peddler, which was documented in 1848 in Hydesville, New York.

Arthur Findlay

Arthur Findlay is a recognized name in the Spiritualist world. He left his home, Stansted Hall, to the Spiritualist National Union (SNU) to be used as a college for the advancement of psychic science; it was renamed the Arthur Findlay College after him. Arthur was a writer, accountant stockbroker, and a magistrate in Essex in the United Kingdom. He had an interest in religions since his parents were Christians, but he diverted away from Christianity to explore comparative religion when he was seventeen. He became interested in spiritualism in 1919 after he had an experience with a medium.

After his experience with the medium John Sloan, Arthur started to pursue spiritualism and came to the conclusion that most gods and other entities that were worshipped in religions were in fact spirits of humans. His interest increased and he founded the Glasgow Society for Psychical Research in 1920. He took part in the Church of Scotland's enquiry into the psychic phenomena in 1923. Psychic studies became his life, and it was in 1932 that he became a founding member of the *Psychic News*, a newspaper that is still in publication today.

Arthur Findlay opened the door for many of us and, through his college, he has made psychic and mediumistic studies acceptable.

Helen Duncan

 One of the most famous Physical Mediums was a woman called Helen Duncan, a Scottish housewife who traveled throughout the United Kingdom during World War II holding séances and providing communication from this world to the next. One of her séances was raided by a plain-clothes police officer who blew his whistle and tried to grab the ectoplasm, claiming that it was a white sheet. The ectoplasm pulled back into the body of the medium extremely quickly so there was nothing that he could grab. Because of her practices she was a threat to the nation in the Second World War, having channeled military personal in once of her many séances, and so she was imprisoned under the 1735 Witchcraft Act. Sir Winston Churchill extremely angry by this and wrote a hand written note to the secretary of state when Helen's case started.

"Give me a report of the 1735 Witchcraft Act.
What was the cost of a trial to the State in which the Recorder
(junior magistrate) was kept busy with all this obsolete tomfoolery
to the detriment of the necessary work in the courts?"

Sadly there was nothing that could be done, with D-Day looming and so Helen served her time and was released in September 1944. The Prime Minister served the spiritual movement well and replaced the Witchcraft Act with the Fraudulent Mediums Act and in 1954 a formal Act of Parliament officially recognized spiritualism as a religion.

However, this didn't stop skeptics, and as Helen was holding another séance, the police raided it. This time the police did the unthinkable to a medium while holding a demonstration: grabbing the medium. This can cause fatal damage. The ectoplasm withdrew quickly back into Helen's body leaving second degree burns across her stomach, and she became so ill she died five weeks later.

It's a sad story, but Helen Duncan was brave and courageous and owned her gift. She surrendered her life to Spirit and provided evidence that life continues on. She never wavered and was proud to do the work that she was placed on this earth to do. She changed the way that people approach spiritualism, certainly within the United Kingdom.

Doris Stokes

Doris Stokes started to see and hear Spirits in her early childhood, just like many of us, and after joining a Spiritual Church in the United Kingdom; she started to develop her gift. Her gifts were very different from Helen's. Helen was a Physical Medium, but Doris used Mental Mediumship. In 1949, she was recognized as a practicing medium under the Spiritualist National Union in the United Kingdom.

Doris decided to pull away from Mediumship but found herself drawn back to this work, understanding that it was her calling in life. Then, in 1975, she became a resident medium at the Spiritualist Association of Great Britain.

She played to sold-out audiences all around the world, brought Mental Mediumship to public attention, and made it acceptable. She became a household name through TV and radio. However, skeptics claimed that she was cold reading—that she had people eavesdropping and gathering information from the audience before the performance and then feeding it to her.

In 1980 she appeared on a British TV show with the magician James Randi who claimed without any evidence that she was a fake and a liar. Doris challenged Randi to appear with her and prove her a fake, but he declined. Sadly, Doris died seven years later after several operations for cancer and one to remove a brain tumor.

Sylvia Browne

Whether you agree or not, we have to pay tribute to Sylvia Browne. Although very controversial in her ways, she changed the way that we view Mediumship and we have to appreciate what she did for the Spiritualist world. Yes, she created some "waves," and society questions the authenticity of her messages, however, the many books that she wrote and her appearances on a popular TV show opened up the views of many and actually brought this work into the present day.

In the beginning she had the compassion and the drive to bring this work forward, and her "couldn't care less" attitude really helped Mediumship become accepted. She didn't care what people thought and continued to deliver messages despite others' opinions. You have to admire that. In recent times, she created controversy with her "predictions" and visions. Until her recent death, she continued to draw in the masses that gathered to watch her talk and give messages from Spirit.

Present Masters

These are mediums who have bought Mediumship forward in a much more acceptable way. They have opened the door, and others in this life have followed them. Many of them were taught the principles of spiritualism in a church and others were taught directly from Spirit, as I was.

There are a few Spiritual Masters that I would like to pay respect to here.

John Edward

John Edward is a recognized name within the Mediumistic world and has brought about a totally fresh approach to this work. He comes across with a friendly but no-nonsense attitude and connects many people to their loved ones on the other side. His popular TV show Crossing Over and his many books are worldwide hits. He gave his first reading at the age of nineteen at a psychic fair and never looked back.

James Van Praagh

Much like John Edward, James Van Praagh brings Mediumship into the eyes of the public with a more modern day approach. His sensitivity and warmth, along with his incredible gift, touch the hearts of many. He has written countless books upon the subject and also produced the popular TV show Ghost Whisperer. He never intended to become a medium, but it was through a reading where he was told he would be doing the work of Spirit that he started to take an interest in meditation, started to "see" things, and started to give readings to friends. He is now one of the world's most respected mediums.

Tony Stockwell

Tony Stockwell started his work at the age of sixteen and has never looked back. He first visited a Spiritual Church and realized that this was what he wanted to dedicate his life too. Spiritualism is part of his soul, and it's who he is. He trained within the SNU and brought Mediumship and psychic awareness into the media with a show called *Street Psychic* where he randomly approached startled people in the street and gave them impromptu readings. He then continued to work on TV and showcased evidential Mediumship at its finest. For me there is no one better to watch than Tony when he gives a message. However, he has been taught through the churches in the United Kingdom and therefore the messages can be cold, hard facts and the healing aspect of Mediumship isn't always evident, especially when you watch some of the TV shows that he has done. But having said that, I have been witness to some of the most amazing healing messages. His wit and humor is not always evident within these readings since he is a pure channel, but he is one of the funniest people I know!

What they all did for Spiritualism

What all of these people have done for the community is open people's eyes to the world beyond and given many courage to "come out" of the "medium closet" and deliver messages from Spirit. This is exactly what has been needed to show society that it can be and should be accepted into the life that we know today.

It hasn't been an easy road, but with strong will and determination they have broken boundaries and helped make this something that is "normal" and "natural." They have taken the "woo woo" out of the work, and more and more people are turning to psychics and mediums. In fact, many of my clients tell me that one session with me has saved them thousands in therapy sessions.

Today's Exercise

In addition to your Connection Meditation in your sacred space, you are going to research and watch some of the masters' work.

Here are my recommendations so that you can experience some delightful connections to the other side.

Doris Stokes, Live at the Barbican—this is a beautiful display of clairaudient Mediumship.

Tony Stockwell—a funny, witty, and charming man who has an astonishing gift of evidential mediumship through claircognizance and clairvoyance.

James Van Praagh—a lovely guy who is a wonderful evidential medium.

There are many videos for Tony Stockwell and James Van Praagh on the Internet, which will show you the wonderful messages that they deliver from Spirit.

You can watch others if you wish, and here are my other recommendations of excellent mediums:

• John Holland   • Mavis Pattilla   • Sharon Klingler

I would also love for you to do some research on a wonderful place called Lily Dale in New York. If you haven't had the pleasure of visiting this quaint community, then I suggest you should. It's the mecca of mediums. In fact many of my courses have been created at the "Inspirational Stump" where thousands of mediums have stood for many years giving messages. It's a gorgeous place that is not only the home of spiritualism in the United States of America but also the world.

Day 11

To start working with Spirit, you have to understand that every Spirit is energy. Spirits no longer have a physical body; therefore they come to us in an energy form. They still have thoughts that they can convey to us, and they can therefore inform us of things that we need to know, but it's done in a more "mental" way. We will be focusing on Mental Mediumship, as it's called, not Physical Mediumship, which is when we physically experience the connection to the afterlife with the things that go "bump in the night." I will explain this more in depth over the next few weeks.

With that said, Mental Mediumship is about energy and how we connect with the energetic Spirit.

Energy

So what is energy? And what does it look like?

All around us is energy of some kind. It could be electrical; it could be natural; but there is energy everywhere. You may have seen energy before but not realized what it was.

Have you ever been outdoors in close proximity to trees, mountains, or the ocean and seen little "blobs" that are transparent but look almost 3-D? Have you ever seen sparkles out of the corners of your eyes and, when you turn to look, you can't see them?

These are some examples of what energy looks like. However, the example I especially like to use, as it's something that most of us have seen, is this: when you look over the hood of a car on a hot day and the heat from the engine and the heat from the air creates a "haze"—that is what energy looks like.

Healers and other spiritual workers may see different forms of energy. The first time I saw light coming from the top of my client's head when I was giving a healing was incredible, but it was just another way that the energy was forming.

So what is energy? Energy is just another word for fuel. We eat to fuel our bodies and keep them working. We turn on the electricity to make appliances work in our homes. But energy is more than that for us.

Think about this situation: Have you ever woken up happy and lively and then suddenly felt low or flat somewhere, perhaps on your way to work or to a meeting? Now think about if you had to stop and fill up your car with gas, you took a phone call, or read a text message or e-mail. You may have absorbed people's energy from interacting with them, and this can have a massive effect on how you feel.

Let me explain more. Everyone has an aura. There are many layers to this aura, and each layer plays an important role. However, it's our energy source. When we are around others our aura intermingles with theirs and that is why you may feel down after you have been in their company.

Take a look at this picture, and you can see a faint line around the person's body. This is the aura, the energy of the person.

We are going to cover the aura next week in depth, but now is the time to experience energy.

Today's Exercise

As well as doing your Connection Meditation in your sacred space, you are going to feel your own energy. I would recommend that you do this *after* you have done your meditation.

- If possible, stand in a comfortable position with your arms relaxed.
- Your feet should be about a shoulder width apart.
- Run your hands together to activate the energy movement within yourself. Your hands may feel a little tingly.
- Bring your arms to your sides, about waist height, outstretched but relaxed with your elbows slightly bent and hands relaxed. Your palms should be facing inward toward each other.
- Gently "bounce" your hands, bringing them closer together.

You will, as your hands reach about a body's width apart, start to feel a resistance with the bounce, and it will be as if your hands are being pushed back, like you are playing with a blown-up beach ball. This is your own natural energy that you are feeling.

It's actually amazing to feel. If you don't feel it at first, *don't worry*. Try again. Don't "think" about it, just allow yourself to relax. The one thing about this work is you can't be too analytical. Just relax and surrender.

Throughout the day, practice this exercise, and you may notice how your energy ball gets bigger or smaller in different situations. If you feel threatened or sad, it will get smaller, and if you are happy and joyous, it will get bigger. It's amazing how you can work with it.

Day 12

As you experienced last week, clearing out a space is vital in order for the energy to move. Your sacred space should be a place that is your haven. Of course you may have to share it with others, but as long as it stays sacred to you, that is what matters. So now you are going to declutter another area of your life.

Many of us spend a lot of time on the computer, and it's become the hub of everything. Social gatherings, news, music, and some of us even watch TV on the computer. So now it's time to clear this up, too.

This is a task that many people dread doing because they dump documents in folders on the desktop, and then they don't clear them up again, like they say they are going too. Our e-mails are not sorted into folders where we can find things easier. Our music is just left in iTunes or another media player, and we find it when we need it.

That is all about to change.

Today's Exercise

You may need to get an external hard drive so that you can put things you don't need on your computer in a safe place. There are many storage facilities online where you store your information on a "cloud" where it's safe and backed up on the Internet. I have my work backed up in both places...one in cloud storage so I can access it anytime and the other on a hard drive. The only reason I use my hard drive is because all my music is stored there and, when I travel internationally, I don't want to use my download capacity for the Internet for streaming music.

So now spend some time decluttering your computer. Place things in files and have them labeled correctly. Delete files that you no longer need to make room for more information, music, and memories.

It's a task that everyone hates to do, but you will feel so much better once it's done. The important thing is to keep it organized from now on!

Before your Connection Meditation, I would like you to start asking Spirit to come forward.

To do this, simply focus on your breath and expand your conscious mind out of your physical body into the space surrounding you. You can also imagine that you have a light coming from the top if your head and it's surrounding your body. The most important thing to remember is to breathe and when you expand your consciousness allow it to expand up and to the side of you.

We expand to the side because we are going to work with the aura, and Spirits connect to parts of our aura and therefore we need to expand outwards to be aware of them. I will cover this more in Day Twenty.

You may have found that you had moments when you questioned the information that you were getting in your head. But now setting the intention for Spirit to come forward is important. It may not happen during this session, but from now on you are going to intend to receive a message or some guidance from the world of Spirit.

Day 13

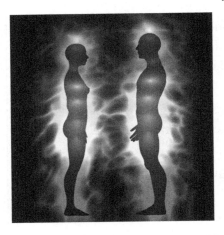

Hopefully you feel fresh and wonderful after decluttering your computer and your meditation. You may start having vivid dreams or start feeling that you need to let go of situations and people in your life. Whatever you are going through is completely *normal,* and I can guarantee that everyone feels the same at this point. You are not alone.

Having support from your friends and family is important. You may find that you are becoming emotional and that you are questioning what you are getting. Don't question anything, just allow things to be. This is part of your spiritual journey and awakening. The more you can do this the better. What you will find is that you are now working internally with your emotions, and it's going to help you connect to Spirit. You are starting to connect slowly, which is important. There is a saying, "don't run before you can walk," and I am teaching you from the basics so that you have a good foundation and this can continue.

We are going to feel energy today. It's a very simple and easy exercise to do. Energy is very important to us all, and if we don't acknowledge it or are not able to feel it, then we really are very detached from this world.

Today's Exercise

You will need to find someone who will help you with this exercise.

Stand behind your friend, who should be sitting comfortably and relaxed.

You are going to feel your friend's energy, and to do this you will use your hands but *do not touch your friend's body*. To feel the energy, you need to start with your hands about a foot above your friend's head. Slowly lower your hands (you may wish to close your eyes as you may find it easier to feel the energy) until you feel a "bounce" or some pressure pushing against your hands. When you feel this bounce, follow it around the body. You are now feeling your friend's energy.

There are also other things that you can do to practice working with and feeling auras without the aid of a friend.

You can try looking at your feet or hands and seeing if you can see the energy or your aura coming from your own body.

To do this, you start looking about two inches above your toes or fingers. When you can see the "haze" of the aura, let your eyes rest there for a while as you just take in the energy.

Then you can follow the energy around your hand or foot.

This exercise is something that I advise you do daily for seven days. The more you practice, the easier it will be for you to see.

Now you are going to go around parts of the house and feel the energy. Go into the bathroom and feel the energy—just stand and feel if it's heavy or light. Go to the bedroom and feel the energy in there. Go around the different parts of the house and connect with this energy, and you will notice that the darker rooms with less light have heavier energy.

As you walk around, I would like you to feel for any presence of energy, meaning a Spirit. I don't want this to alarm you, and you have lived with Spirits coming in and out of your home all your life; they won't harm you. It's our imaginations that create the problems. We overthink too much. But the reality is that they have probably been there all along.

When you start to acknowledge Spirits, they become a little more active because you are accepting their existence, but it will be "normal" things that you have experienced before.

Don't worry. They will *not* harm you. Spirits are everywhere.

Don't forget your Connection Meditation today!

Day 14—Review Day

1. What did you find most fascinating about the history of spiritualism, and did you know about the history before reading this book?

2. What other mediums did you decide to watch, and why? What did you enjoy about their work?

3. When you were feeling the energy around your home, what did you discover?

4. Did you like working with the energy, and how did it make you feel?

5. Describe any unusual or interesting meditation experiences.

6. Did you discover that you hoarded a great number of things around your house and computer? How does it make you feel now that you are decluttering slowly?

Well done on completing Week Two. Next week we are going to be taking our understanding of energy further, and we will be getting to know the body and protecting our surrounding areas. We will also be connecting more to Spirit.

WELCOME TO WEEK *Three*

This week it is important for you to understand the way that your body works energetically. Last week we explored energy and how you can feel and see it, but this week I am going to show you how to work with it and how your body is associated with energy.

It's going to be a lovely week for you, as you will also start connecting with your own loved ones in the Spirit World. They are waiting to connect with you, and some of them have patiently been waiting for this time so that you will be fully prepared and able to connect in the best possible way. Just remember to take each day at a time and don't rush. Each day has been strategically planned out for you so that you are not overwhelmed and you can learn in the best possible way. Please continue to reduce your media and "exits" that you use to "escape" life so you can be more present.

Being present is going to help you connect to your loved ones. Notice how many times you habitually go to your phone and look at your e-mails or Facebook, especially if you haven't deleted all the social media apps that you have on there....

If you feel that this is you, then watch your routine. Is it when you are quiet and alone that you open your phone and then tap on Facebook or Twitter? You may notice that you have a routine. For example, you jump from Facebook to Twitter and then to Instagram and then to your e-mails. These are signs that you can't or don't want to be present in your life and that you are trying to "escape"... what you are trying to escape from is something that only you will know. Maybe you don't like to be alone, maybe you like to be connected, maybe you have to be in touch with everything that is going on in the world, or maybe you need to be needed. Whatever it is, then it's your feeling, but you have to "own" the fact that you are doing it and then stop.

Your ego is getting to you, and this is something you can ill afford to have happen when you are working on connecting to Spirit.

So be present, and if you find that you are reaching for social media, *stop* and think about what is going on in your world that you need to escape. Maybe it's actually being alone and you need to escape your own thoughts. If necessary use your journal to help you write about your feelings.

Day 15

So as we prepare for the first day, you need to be aware that you have the ability to connect to your loved ones; you just need to be *open* and ready to connect. You may think that you are ready, but mate, you are "telling" yourself that you are and are actually really scared. Well you are here for a reason, reading this, so therefore, somewhere deep within you, you are ready. Your subconscious will be raring to connect, but your conscious mind will stop you. Trust me when I say this because you will have days when your mind will play tricks on you, you won't think so highly of yourself, and you will start to tell yourself you can't do it. I know this because it happens to me. It's our insecurity. The insecurity is within us all.

So today you are going to spend some time setting an intention for your daily meditation and then working on your connection to Spirit.

When you set an intention, you are going to be setting what I personally call a trigger for Spirit. This trigger is going to be something that will work for you, and you can then create boundaries with Spirit.

As I have said before think about what you wear most of the time, and when you are ready to connect with Spirit take it off.... Make it a trigger.

For example, my trigger is a watch. I can still give a reading with a watch on, *but* it feels restrictive and I am "aware" of it, where normally I wouldn't be. So if I am sitting in a restaurant and suddenly I am subconsciously taking off my watch, I know that I am connecting with a Spirit. It's funny; when it happens my friends or family say, "Lisa, what are you picking up?" or "Why are you taking off your watch?" People know it. I used to use a hat, but since I often used it to cover bad hair days, I stopped using it as my trigger.

So think about your trigger. It could be a ring that you wear, a bracelet...just about anything.

Another thing you need to be aware of is having any metals around your wrist or on any other energetic outlets on your body when you connect with Spirit. Metals are like magnets to our natural energy and we have thousands of energy centers around the body. It can create blockages when you work with Spirit. Your energy will not flow well. It's important when you start that you understand this. Many mediums have been working with metals on their body for years, but in a recent study of watching established mediums work with and without their jewelry, ninety five percent of them said that they connected better and in a stronger way with Spirit. So take your time to take these off. Again this could naturally be your trigger if you do wear them.

Today's Exercise

In your sacred space I would like you to place a small tray or box so that it triggers you to automatically take off any jewelry when you work and so that you know that your jewelry is safe while you work.

Now you are going to set an intention for your meditations this week.

In your journal I would like you to write about the person that you want to connect with. Please write about:

- what the person looks like
- how old the person was
- the person's likes and dislikes
- the person's favorite music
- what the person's passions in life were

For this exercise, imagine that you are writing to a friend about the person that you want to connect with.

Place the person's photograph, if you have one, close to you as you sit in your sacred space, and set an intention for your meditation. The intention should be something like "I will remain calm and relaxed and embrace all connections to the afterlife that I make through this meditation."

This will help you. You can say it out loud three times, or you can write it three times. I don't want you to say, "I am asking to connect with (person's name) during this meditation." The reason is you are setting expectations, and you will only be disappointed if it doesn't happen. What you have to realize is that you are going to be connecting to Spirit over the next few days and you will eventually make connections to your loved ones.

Now, you are going to sit in your sacred space and sit quietly allowing your consciousness to expand and see if you can sense Spirit drawing close to you. Ask for your loved ones to come forward to connect with you. This is your mediation to connect with your loved ones. Please ensure that you remain in that space for at least 15 minutes to ensure that you relax, Spirit will connect easier when you are relaxing.

Please document all the signs and messages that you receive in your journal.

Day 16

This week we are also focusing on what I call the **cycle of protection**, and every medium, psychic, healer, and spiritual worker should understand this cycle, since it's important. I refer to the cycle of protection a lot, because it's how our "self" takes care of each element of our energetic make up.

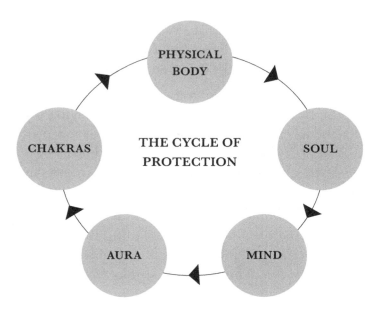

The body is a vessel that is vitally important to us in this cycle, and each element is as important as the next. Over the next few days, we will look at each element in this cycle individually so you can understand it. The body houses the soul, which means that the body needs to stay healthy to continue the journey that we are supposed to live. We need to take care of it. Energy gets trapped within our bodies and we feel sluggish, lethargic, and we don't want to do anything, so we need to move our bodies daily.

Yes, exercise *is* important; it not only keeps us fit, active, and healthy, but it facilitates letting go of built-up energy. You don't have to do much to move the energy around your body, but you need to do *something*.

Daily, you need to move your arms around, move your body, and walk. Whatever you decide to do, it will help you to move the energy.

Today's Exercise

Create a routine of exercise. Whether it is walking daily, yoga, or something more heavy duty, start it today! It doesn't have to be much, but it needs to get the energy moving.

It's time to look at the food that you eat. What you consume is important for your connection. I am not saying that you have to be a vegan, but do be aware of any heavy processed foods that are in your diet, excess sugar, and fast foods. Look at your diet and really consider what you are prepared to give up.

Now I can tell you that I used to eat meat, but I never ate red meat three days before any reading (which basically meant I never ate red meat...hehe!), and when I am on tour, I primarily ate fish. This is what I need for my diet. I am now a vegan, gluten free and soy free, I do have the occasional glass of wine but I do not drink much alcohol. I eat mainly organic foods and, if possible, nothing processed. I also avoid a lot of sugar, and I never drink soda.

This is something that works for me and I have found my connection to Spirit much more finely tuned and it is easier to connect.

So now examine your diet and see what needs changing. Go through your cupboards in the kitchen and decide what you need and what you can throw away.

Throw away any out-of-date foods that you have and stock your kitchen with healthy food this week. If necessary, plan your meals.

For the final exercise today, you need to stand in a mirror, ideally full length, and examine your body. I want you to put your hands on the areas of your body that you don't like and start to love and appreciate them.

Your body is so important in the cycle of protection since it houses the soul. It's the vessel that has been given to you to carry you through life, so appreciate and love it.

If you wish to change it, then that is your prerogative, *but* you are beautiful just the way you are, and you need to believe that in order to get full balance of mind, body, and soul.

Please don't forget your mediation with your loved ones and to set the intention before you connect with them.

Day 17

As we already discussed, the body houses and protects the soul. The soul is *who we are*. It's the very essence of our being. We decided our pathway in life before we came to the earth plane; therefore we are doing everything that is right for us in life.

Now some would say that the soul is connected to the subconscious mind, and to a degree it is. Our subconscious mind knows our plan but the conscious mind doesn't.

The soul is something that we have to honor and love. And we need to appreciate who we are as souls. This is something that is good for us. In many respects we need to have a clear conscience about many things. Often we seek forgiveness. But most of the time, we need to seek forgiveness from ourselves. Whatever you have done in life you will find that some people have forgiven you but you are holding onto guilt. It's time to stop.

When your soul feels free, it can help protect the mind, which is the next step in the cycle.

So today I would like you to think about what needs to be released from your soul for you to be free.

You may need to say sorry to someone. Release yourself from the guilt.

In some instances you may not be able to speak to the people to make amends, but you can write letters to them and release your emotions. If you wish, you can send them to them.

You may feel like you need to be heard, and so it's time to start voicing your thoughts and feelings.

Here are some suggestions for you:

- Write a journal. Every time you have guilt toward "something" or "someone," write in the journal and forgive yourself.

- Write a list of people whom you need to voice your opinions, thoughts, and feelings to and ask to meet with them and speak the truth.

- Remain authentic all day with your emotions and how you interact with people.

- Purge your emotions in a journal, and allow yourself to really *feel* your feelings.

- Allow yourself to cry. Whatever the reason for your tears, you need to know it's **OK**, perfectly natural, and *healthy*.

These are just some suggestions. You may find your own ways to cleanse your soul that are more effective. Somehow you need to feel as though you are lightening your soul's load and allowing it to be free.

Today's Exercise

Start making a list of things that you need to release from your soul and then start the process. This is going to be an ongoing exercise and one that, on some days, you won't like. However, allowing yourself to be free is essential for your growth spiritually, and it will then make it easier for you when it comes to protecting your mind, which is what the soul does.

Please don't forget your meditation to connect with your loved ones.

Day 18

Your mind is constantly active, no matter what situation you find yourself in. When you are sleeping, your mind processes the day's events.

The mind is split into two parts: the conscious mind and the subconscious mind.

As I have said, the subconscious mind is attached to the soul, however, the soul protects the mind. Let me explain why.

When we have trauma, such as a severe car accident, we tend to "shut it away," and we don't consciously remember what happened. It gets locked away in the subconscious, and the soul holds the knowledge and will only allow you to consciously remember when you are ready. So the soul protects your conscious mind from knowing the trauma before you can deal with it emotionally.

The soul is extremely strong and can never be broken, and so it can hold a great deal of information and release it when you need it. Look at how many times you have had to pick yourself up when times were hard. You didn't break, you grew stronger.

However, your mind is powerfully energetic, and it's amazing what we can manifest when we put our energy into our thoughts. That's why the mind is used to protect the aura, which is around the body. The mind can protect the aura just by the power of thought, but the mind also has to be decluttered and free. It's quite interesting when you think about how much balancing of the mind, body, and soul it takes to help the connection with Spirit. Finding the balance with it all is a constant thing in my life …but it's become habitual, and now it's how I live my life constantly. It's become the norm for me.

The one thing that we fight with daily in our conscious mind is the way that it "talks" to us. The alter ego. I call it Veronica. When we are quiet, we have thoughts that race through our minds that we sometimes struggle with. We often tell ourselves that we are not good enough or that we shouldn't do something. It's our own insecurities that come into play. To be free from them is important…or should I say be free from the control of Veronica!

It's never easy, and everyone in the world will have some doubt at one time or another, but in order for us to have the purity of mind to get the clarity of protection that we need for our aura, we need to alleviate the alter ego from getting in the way.

Today's Exercise

You are going to name the little voice in your head. If you can, I would like you to detach from your alter ego and watch how it talks to you…but I don't want you to analyze anything that it says. Watch how it talks negatively to you about some situations in your life. You will often find the best place for this to come out is when you are showering as the thoughts race through your mind. This is going to be a twenty-four-hour exercise that, trust me, you are going to want to continue for the rest of your life.

So whenever you hear those negative thoughts, I would like you to listen to them as if you were listening to a friend, and know that they are just talking negative and that you shouldn't believe it all. Watch how your alter ego creates drama that you don't need in your life.

Also connect with your loved ones today through your meditation. You will find that they are getting closer and closer the more that you do this.

Day 19

Today we are going to examine the aura. You already connected with your friend's aura and energy last week, but now you are going to understand the importance of it. You don't need to know everything about the aura, but what you do need to know is that it's extremely important to the energy flow of the body and how you connect to Spirit.

Have you ever felt drained after being around people all day or got on a flight and suddenly felt exhausted? This is because you are absorbing all the energy from your surrounding areas, and your body is finding it too much to cope with. You are on an energy overload, and then you want to sleep, or you walk away feeling drained. It's because your body has done everything to fight the energy that you don't need.

We absorb energy through the aura. The reason why the mind

protects the aura is because the mind is powerful and can create and imagine many things. So when you become overloaded with energy, you imagine a shield of protection surrounding you; suddenly you can feel like you are locked away from the world and that nothing can harm you. It's a magical feeling. I do it all the time. I feel like I am cocooned in this energetic space and nothing can penetrate it.

If you don't do this protection, you will get energy vampires. When you do this work, everyone wants to be your best friend, and they will all "take" from you, so you need to protect yourself. So use your mind to protect yourself.

Let me also explain a little about why we use the aura to connect with Spirit. The aura has several layers, as you can see in this picture.

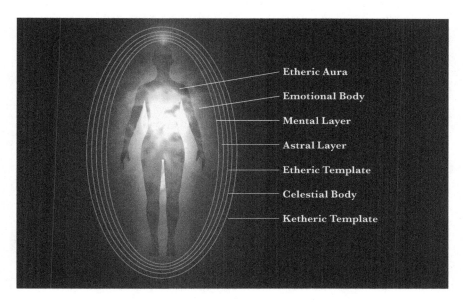

In our studies, the most important layer is the etheric template, which is an exact replica of the etheric aura. As you can see in the diagram above the etheric template is further out in the aura in what is called the 'spiritual layer' of the aura, and it's where the

Spirits can penetrate and connect with us. Whatever we feel on the etheric template is also felt on the etheric aura, that's why we "feel" Spirit and connect with them. They will stand behind you, and you turn and look but no one will be there. Well, they are, but you can't see them. You will find that this will come in handy when we start to work with our senses.

There are other layers of the aura, and while it is nice to know about them, it's not essential at this stage.

Today's Exercise

First of all you are going to learn protection. With the power of the mind you are going to imagine that you are inside a thick glass cube. Don't forget that it needs to go under your feet. That way it will protect you completely. When you do this, you will feel totally protected, however, you do need to repeat this three times a day. So for the rest of the book, when you connect, you are going to ensure that you are protecting yourself completely.

Now I would like you to sit in your sacred space, and just before your meditation I want you to imagine that you are pushing your aura out as far as you can go. Imagine that your consciousness is being extended as far as you can, imagine pushing it out to the edges of the room that you are sitting in and beyond and then sit…and start your meditation.

While you are meditating, I want you to think about what you are feeling and picking up from your body. You may find that some parts of the body start to hurt or ache, maybe because your loved ones had issues in those areas, too, before they passed over. Please don't worry about it. As my grandmother said, "If they didn't hurt you while they were alive then they will not hurt you when they are dead" and she was right!

Day 20

The chakras are last in the cycle of protection. The aura protects the chakras energetically so that the chakras continue to spin and work to maintain the healthy life force that is needed in the body.

There are many different chakras on the body, but we are going to focus on the major chakras. There are seven major chakras that flow through your body, and they are about four inches in diameter and come out of the front and the back of the body. They send energy to the vital organs in your body to keep them healthy. So as you can see, it's important for your aura to protect your chakras from any negative energy that comes into your energy field.

Each chakra has a specific color attached to it and is associated with a different part of the body. As you can see in the diagram, there are many properties to the chakras. It's worth really sitting and reading this diagram. Your chakras should *never* be closed. If you are ever told to close a chakra, that person is telling you to cut off vital energy to your body that keeps the organs healthy and alive.

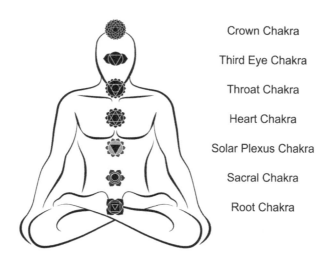

Crown Chakra

Third Eye Chakra

Throat Chakra

Heart Chakra

Solar Plexus Chakra

Sacral Chakra

Root Chakra

The Major Chakras

	1st Chakra Root	2nd Chakra Sacral	3rd Chakra Solar Plexus
Color	Red	Orange	Yellow
Character	Physical vitality and survival	Desires, which also include sexual energy and our feelings	Creation of self, perception and projection of self
Location	Base of the spine, out of the body and a 45-degree angle	Center of abdomen	Between the belly button and breast bone
Parts of the body it governs	Skeletal system (bones and teeth) Prostate glands Lymph system Bladder and elimination system Lower parts of the body, legs, feet and ankles Adrenal glands Nasal passage	Reproductive areas Sexual organs Lower back	Muscular system Skin Large intestine Stomach Organs and glands in the solar plexus Liver Eyes and face Metabolism
Association	Any tension here will make you feel insecure	Helps with the ability to change our life	Brings us energy and rules personal power. If you feel trapped in life, this area will feel tight
Element	Earth	Water	Fire and Sun
Sound	C	D	E
Crystals	Agate Bloodstone Hematite Garnet Ruby Red jasper	Carnelian Coral Amber Citrine Gold topaz Moonstone	Citrine Gold topaz Amber Tiger's eye

4th Chakra Heart	5th Chakra Throat	6th Chakra Brow	7th Chakra Crown
Green	Blue	Indigo / Purple	Violet
Universal love, empathy and creation	Communication and creative expression	Visualisation and psychic awareness	Spirituality
Center of the chest	Base of the throat	Between your eyes, mid brow area	Top of your head
Heart Circulation system Lungs Chest area Thymus gland Controlling the immune system	Throat Neck Arms Hands Thyroid	Forehead Temples Pituitary gland Eyes	Nervous system Lower brain Pineal gland
This chakra is often closed because of emotional traumas. Hugging can stimulate this chakra.	Associated with intuition. It can cause neck, shoulder and throat problems and an underactive thyroid	Deep inner being of self Being in touch with your soul	Spiritual development. Meditation will help open this chakra. Allows messages and guidance from Spirit.
Air	Air	Light and Water	Fire and Thought
F	G	A	B
Emerald Green tourmaline Malachite Green jade Green aventurine Rose quartz Ruby Fluorite	Turquoise Blue sapphire Blue topaz Sodalite Lapis Aquamarine	Lapis Fluorite Sodalite Clear quartz Sapphire	Amethyst Purple fluorite Clear quartz Diamond

Today's Exercise

If you read these questions, you can see which chakras are blocked, and then you can open them. You may wish to use crystals and place them on each individual chakra point so that the points open and the energy flows. You may wish to visualize the specific colors of each chakra: imagine vibrant color flowing in to the area and spinning freely. If you can do this with every chakra, then they will be open and flowing. They need this to protect the body. Or you can listen to the provided guided meditation to help you.

For you to work to the best of your ability, you need to ensure that your chakras are balanced. But sometimes it's hard to determine which chakras need to be worked on. This next exercise will help you determine these chakras.

Can you answer *yes* to any of these questions?

- Do you find that you feel unsafe in some situations?
- Do you suffer with depression or have contemplated suicide?
- Do you have physical pain in your joints or back?
- Is money a constant stress for you that causes anxiety?
- Do you find that you have problems using the bathroom?

If you answered yes, you need to work on your Root Chakra.

Can you answer *yes* to any of these questions?

- Do you find it difficult to be intimate?
- Are you wishing to change things in your life but finding it difficult?
- Do you shy away from your true feelings?
- Do you find it hard to live in the moment?

- Do you feel that you are emotionally insecure?

If you answered yes, then you need to work on your Sacral Chakra.

Can you answer *yes* to any of these questions?

- Are you searching for your life's purpose?
- Do you worry about what people think about you?
- Do your muscles ache even when you haven't been doing something strenuous?
- Do you struggle spending time alone?
- Do you find it hard to make decisions?

If you answered yes, then you need to work on your Solar Plexus Chakra.

Can you answer *yes* to any of these questions?

- Do you feel that you are emotionally disconnected in life?
- Are you constantly trying to please everyone?
- Do you struggle accepting who you are as a person?
- Do you suffer from a tight chest or problems breathing?
- Do you fear rejection?

If you answered yes, then you need to work on your Heart Chakra.

Can you answer *yes* to any of these questions?

- Do you find it hard to voice your opinions?
- Do you have swelling in your Neck, Shoulders, Arms or hands?
- Do you lack trust in other people?
- Are you unorganized?
- Do you worry about your financial situation?

If you answered yes, then you need to work on your Throat Chakra.

Can you answer *yes* to any of these questions?

- Do you have psychic visions and don't tell others?

- Can you be judgmental?

- Do you find it hard to meditate?

- Are you negative in life?

- Do you suffer with headaches across your forehead?

If you answered yes, then you need to work on your Brow Chakra.

Can you answer *yes* to any of these questions?

- Do you crave attention from others?

- Do you feel that you are disconnected spiritually?

- Do you lack a sense of purpose in life?

- Do you suffer with anxiety?

- Are you longing for a sign from your loved one but haven't seen one?

If you answered yes, then you need to work on your Crown Chakra.

If you have found that any one of your chakras are blocked or closed then you need to spend time working on them. I suggest you first bathe in an Epsom salts bath for about 20 minutes and then, if you have some of the crystals that have been suggested in the chakra chart on Page 72 – 73, you can place the crystals associated with each chakra on your body at each of the chakra points for a further 20 minutes.

If you do not have the crystals you can imagine that you are breathing in the different colors into each individual chakra. This will activate the chakra.

Ensuring that your Chakras are open is essential for you.

And so the cycle begins again…

- The chakras protect the body.
- The body protects the soul.
- The soul protects the mind.
- The mind protects the aura.
- The aura protects the chakras.

Don't forget to do your meditation today.

Hopefully you are starting to connect with Spirit or noticing signs that they are around you.

Day 21—Review Day

1. Did you find that you had a connection to your loved one during your meditations this week?

2. Please explain what you believe the cycle of protection is, and why it's important.

3. Did you notice the change in energy when you were more aware of your energetic make up?

4. Which part of the aura is important to connect with when you are working with Spirit, asking for a connection, and why?

5. What chakras did you discover needed some work, and how did you go about opening them up?

WELCOME TO WEEK *Four*

I hope that you were able to make some connections to your loved ones this last week through your meditations. It's extremely powerful to be able to connect with your loved ones yourself. Many people believe that they need a medium to connect, but actually they don't. You just need some time, patience, and space. Then let the magic begin! Now I must stress that there is a huge difference between seeing the signs that your loved ones are around you and becoming a medium. Trust me. A medium is someone who will be able to deliver messages to you from your loved ones with accuracy. But when your loved ones are connecting with you directly it's because they want to connect, and they love you.

Now I do want to state here that if you didn't connect with your loved ones, then please know that is normal for the first try. Don't be disappointed. You are just starting out. You have to trust and believe.

The key to this work is actually allowing your mind to completely surrender beyond what you know, beyond what you believe is right and wrong, beyond into a realm where anything is possible. We put limitations on ourselves in our minds when actually we shouldn't. We shouldn't put limitations on anything. When we don't limit ourselves, we stop surrendering. So surrender to the fact that whatever happens is going to happen, and stop the control.

When you release all control you can connect in such a powerful way.

When writing this, I sat and thought about this week a great deal because having to commit to exercises daily and doing all the work can be hard when you have a busy life, and I did contemplate giving you a few days off. But then I thought why not, let's keep the momentum going. I know that you may be feeling the strain or pressure, and that is normal. You have probably started to discover a lot about yourself and your life, and this is great. You are letting go of things that you don't need. You may have discovered that you are not ready for this, and you are putting it aside for a later date. If that is the case, then it's OK. You will find that you will learn when the time is right for you. Never let anyone force you into a situation that you don't want to do. However, if you do decide that you are going to let it go for a while, when you do pick it up again, please go back to the beginning as it's going to help you make your connections stronger.

Day 22

Thinking back to your meditations last week, I would like you to notice how they made an impact on you. You may have discovered so much about yourself and your life. Sitting in meditation is so powerful, and this is why I mentioned that you might decide to drop this book for a little while. The meditations can spark new ideas, connections, and self-discoveries. It's incredible when you start to do it.

Today is a day of reflection. It's a day of appreciation for you and what you have discovered in your meditation. You may have connected to one important person, or you may have connected to many. You may have had a situation where one day the mediation was so powerful that you had that connection with your loved one, and it was so intense that you wanted to experience that all the time. You may not have connected with your loved one, but you may have connected with a Spirit Guide, someone who can guide you through your life. Or you may have just had quiet solitude to connect to yourself, which has been powerful, and you have gained a greater understanding of who you are.

Whatever you discovered in your meditations is right for you. Things will surface as and when they need to come up. If you remember back to last week I said the soul will only give the conscious mind what it needs at this time to function, especially in traumatic situations, so you only get what you can handle You are never overloaded. We, as conscious humans, overload ourselves; we need to make life simple.

Today's Exercise

It's time to sit and reflect and write in your journal.

Sit in your sacred space with your journal and pen and just write. Allow your mind to be free and reflect on your journey so far. Write everything that you have experienced, noticed, and felt while you have been on this journey. Allow yourself the honor to bring everything alive. Spend time noticing how you have changed and how you feel about this. Just sit with your emotions.

You have done an amazing job, and now it's time for you to appreciate your journey.

Day 23

 As I have said before, this journey really is going to spark so many emotions within you, and whatever you feel, it's OK. What you have to stop doing is being hard on yourself. You need to allow your mind to be free from thoughts of "I should be doing..." or "I'm sorry, I can't seem to do...." This is your own impression of what you believe people need and expect. Well, it's time to release that. Disappointment comes from expectations; so don't have any expectations from now on. These expectations can cause us to be disappointed. We put expectations on ourselves, and so we disappoint ourselves. It's time to release this. Stop that and live in the now with the acceptance that what we are experiencing is right for us now.

This is actually hard to do sometimes because we have been conditioned to follow society and put on a brave face and deal with life. Well, we don't have to do that. I want to talk about grief here. Grief is exceptionally important to deal with, and no one likes to talk about it or deal with it. It's been something that, for many years, they have put behind them or swept under the carpet. Well, it's time to *stop*.

I want you to think about this for a moment. How many times have you watched people cry and handed them a tissue to "wipe away the tears?" Many times. I know I have; it's a natural thing to do. We think that we are helping people so that they don't mess up their makeup or their nose doesn't run. Well, think about this: what we are doing is telling them to wipe away those tears. It's something that we need to stop doing. We always hate to see people cry, but it's one of the most natural things to do. Crying is a release of emotion, it's wonderful. Allowing ourselves to cry is powerful and can release so much.

Now I am not saying not to dry your own tears if you don't want to—because if you do, then that's OK—but allow yourself to use a few boxes of tissues if you need too. It's OK. But if people are crying, allow them to cry and don't immediately go comfort or hug them. Give them space to have the emotion that they need. You can certainly place boxes of tissues near them, but let them get their own. You need to give people space to cry and just be. It's one of the most powerful emotions of being completely present. Don't crowd their space, just sit. Don't offer a solution, just listen. Don't try to make things better, because you can't, and this is something that they have to go through.

On the flip side, grief is a powerful space to be in. You are allowing your emotions and your self to be present and go through a grieving process.

For me, as a medium it's important for my clients to have as much grieving time as possible, so I don't read for anyone who has had a recent death. When someone dies, people are so desperate to make the connection, but the reality is they need to grieve, or they will rely on the medium for that connection to their loved ones. That is when I have a psychic junkie on my hands, which isn't healthy. I've been there before...I *was* that psychic junkie.

It's not a good space to be in, and so I try to create healthy boundaries. The reality is that we have to cope without that person around us anymore, and we have to learn to do that on our own. When you have had three months of getting into that space of being "OK," then I'm comfortable in giving that reading to help with the closure; until then, you can't process it.

There are five stages of grief that we go through. I want to just make it clear that I am not only talking about death; I am also talking about the loss of a relationship, a job, an animal, just about anything that has upset you emotionally to the point that you have cried or gotten upset. Some grief will be stronger than others.

Obviously reading this book will have sparked some emotions of loss again for certain people in your life, so now you have to understand it, and this is what we are going to work on this week: helping you understand your grief and emotions.

Elisabeth Kübler-Ross is an amazing author on the subject of grief. Her book *On Grief and Grieving* is incredibly powerful, and I would recommend that anyone who is grieving should read it. She talks about the five stages of death.

Denial—"I'm fine."

You don't want to believe that it's happening, and it's like a dream to you that you have lost someone. You want to wake up and discover it's all a dream. You will not want to accept the reality that your loved one has gone. This is not a good time for you to have a reading because you can't believe that it's happened.

Anger—"Why me?" "It's not fair!" "Who is to blame?"

You will express this anger and will look for other people to blame or look for other excuses. It's typical and very normal. You will have anger and rage within you that you may not know how to control or where it's come from. You are angry because the person that you love has gone. This is when you hear "If there were a god, he wouldn't allow this to happen." People's faith changes in this process.

When people are in this stage, I don't recommend a reading, *but* I will say it's up to them. The reason is they will not want to accept the information that I give them, particularly if it was a suicide. They start to look for every possible excuse for someone else killing their loved ones.

Bargaining— "I'll do anything for one more conversation."

This is when you start to think that you could have done something to change this happening. "If only I had done this or that." You start to bargain with yourself or god, saying, "If I do this, will you bring her back?" It's hard when this is happening, but this is a time when a reading can have a major healing impact on your life. It will show you that it was your loved one's time to pass, and there was nothing that could be done. It doesn't make it better, but you may understand more.

Having a reading at this time doesn't mean that you are "healed" and have closure, but what it does mean is that the next stages may be easier.

Depression—
"Why bother?" "I just want to be with them."

The thing to know here is that you will not change this depression, not with a reading or anything. You will have a moment of happiness and connection, but you will not be miraculously healed. This is something that you have to do and will do. It's natural for us all to feel emotions of sadness and loss, and it's also healthy for us since we are getting to the next stage of acceptance now that our loved ones have passed.

During this stage a reading can help you. You will be able to reflect on the reading to reestablish the connection with your loved one, and it will help you through your darkest moments of pain and loss.

Acceptance—
"It's going to be OK." "Things happen for a reason."

This is when you accept the situation that your loved one has crossed on and that you are a person with a life to lead. The widowed start to date, people start to laugh and have fun, and they just want to know that their loved ones are OK with them enjoying their lives.

This is an excellent time for a reading as it will help you know that your loved ones are OK with you moving forward and will actually help you in your life. You get acknowledgement that it's

OK to make new friends, have new relationships, or have another child. You start to see how beautiful life can be, and the reading is a remarkable healing process that can give so much closure.

Today's Exercise

It's a time to just be present. Having thought about all of these emotions, you may realize that you are still in a stage of grief. You may realize that you that you are stronger than you give yourself credit for. You may also realize how far you have actually come. You may also be someone fortunate enough to have not lost someone, but realize that you have this gift and the knowledge to help others who may grieve around you, if you decide that you want to be a medium.

Think about how far you have come, and how you handled the grief that you went through. Today is a day of being present!

Day 24

Still keeping to our theme, your loved ones are always around you. They don't watch you in the shower or using the bathroom; there is an unspoken rule that this doesn't happen. But whenever you need them and reach out to them, then they will be there. When your loved ones "pop" into your head randomly, it means that they are there to support you and are helping and guiding you. So just know that they are *always* there for you.

You are not holding them back on their journey through the afterlife: they want to help you. They have time, and they can come and connect with you. Their world moves much faster than ours. Remember they don't need eight hours of sleep like we do, so they can accomplish so much more than we can. Their healing is faster than ours.

Our healing is essential. You want to connect to your loved ones. You may have something you wish to say. Now is the time to connect with them on a conscious level.

Today's Exercise

You are now going to write letters to whom you need to express emotions to. Whatever you need to say or do is going to be right. Remember that there are no right or wrong feelings. You just have to honor how you feel. You may wish to sit and meditate on this for a while, or you may want to just write and see what comes out. Do whatever you wish to do.

Think about who you want to say things to and then write to that individual. Allow your heart to pour out, and if you cry, it's OK. These are your letters. I get many people to do this exercise, and they continue it for a long time. It's a great exercise if you miss people and you just want to connect with them. You can even just write about your day as if you were talking to them. Whatever it is, just write.

Imagine that you are talking to them and allow the words to flow.

Some people wish to *send* those letters, and if that is the case, then you can. You can send them to a friend. Family member or even yourself. Whatever you decide is right for you.

Have a beautiful day.

Day 25

Have you noticed you have not had to do any meditations? This is because, hopefully, you have gotten into a routine of meditation. However, it is also because I was "told" (from Spirit) when writing this book that you need to be consciously present when dealing with these last few days. While meditation would have helped, I am always guided by Spirit, so I had to allow that to happen. But this is when the meditation has to start again.

There is no harm in having a few days off now and then. It's like when you are on a diet, occasionally giving yourself the treat that you want or feel you deserve…you can have it!

Within your meditations this week, *you* are the focus. It's for you and your soul. You are going to go through a time of reflection and allow yourself to appreciate who you are. It's been an intense week so far, although that certainly wasn't my intention. And as always, being guided by Spirit is something that I have to embrace. Spirit always knows what you want and need.

So having said that, the meditation is about you. You are going to connect to your soul. It's about reflecting on your life and who you are.

Today's Exercise

Sit in your sacred space and allow peace to wash over you as you are guided through this meditation. Please use your journal to take any notes after your meditation.

Enjoy!

Day 26

Self-appreciation time. It's so powerful to really see who you are through someone else's eyes. This week has sparked so many emotions, and you may have thought, "I can't do this." Well you can! You have to go through self-healing with everything that you do in life because it's going to be incredible when you connect to Spirit. You need to be a clear channel, which is why clutter doesn't work in a room, especially in your sacred space. Having lots of emotions that you haven't dealt with is going to limit your experience.

It's like what I said at the beginning of the week: you need to surrender to whatever you get. I have a saying, "You get what you get and don't be upset." You should never be upset with the information or knowledge that you get; you need to embrace it. Obviously that saying doesn't apply to everything, but it certainly does when it comes to receiving information from Spirit.

Today is a wonderful day. You are going to contact ten people you know. They need to be a mixture of friends, family, and acquaintances, and they need to be honest and authentic with what they give you. I would like you to ask them to each give you five words that describe you as a person.

You are going to see yourself through someone else's eyes. It's a remarkable thing to see yourself how others see you.

Today's Exercise

Ask ten people to give you five words to describe you as a person. Some people may give you the same words, and that is OK. While you are waiting for those words to be given to you, you are also going to come up with your own five words for yourself.

Now you are going to write your own eulogy. A eulogy is a speech that someone gives at a funeral about the deceased's life.

Your eulogy is going to include all of the words that you were given as well as the five you came up with. You will write about your life and who you are as a person. It's a powerful exercise if you can do it. It will bring out some emotions, *but* it will hopefully help you understand who you are as a person and what you bring to other peoples' lives. I always believe that when you write something so powerful, it should be shared, so consider reading it to a friend.

Day 27

It's the final day of your self-care week, and now you are going to release any fears and start to step into belief. If I had a magic wand, I would wave it over you; however, I can't. All I can do is give you the tools so you can do this yourself. Now that you have seen what people think about you, you are going to look at yourself clearly. Sometimes, by staring into our own eyes, we can really see who we are. Having written your own eulogy, you can see what others think of you, and now you can release any fear that you have and start to believe in yourself.

Today's Exercise

You are going to take those words that were given to you by your friends, family, and acquaintances, and you are going to go and stand in front of the mirror. You are going to lean into the mirror really close so that you can see the color of your eyes so clearly that you can see the tiny flecks of color around your pupil. Really stare into your eyes and see into your soul. Just stand looking at yourself for one minute. It will seem like forever, but just stand there. If you can, try to look into a mirror in which you can see your whole face and not just your eyes.

After the first minute, you are going to keep staring into that mirror, but you are going to say every word that you received. Say them as if you mean them. Honor everything that you have been given. This is how people see you. How others see you. It's time to believe in yourself and who you are.

Next you are going to sit in your sacred space and write down all the things that you fear...and why. I want you to look at them from a third-person point of view and realize that they are not to be feared and they will only make you stronger.

It's time to release them, and you may wish to burn them or rip them up into tiny pieces and throw them away. Whatever you decide is right for you. You need to let go of these and be present.

It's time to meditate!

Its time to sit in a comfortable position and just be, just love yourself and honor who you are. You don't have to do anything except be with yourself. The world will continue to revolve while you take time out.

Close your eyes and start to focus on your breath. Allow your breath to penetrate to your core and start to honor the emotions that are with in you.

Connect with yourself and your settle in that space and allow yourself to surrender to your soul.

Remember to continue to reduce media and all other escapes and just focus on *you*!

You are incredible and beautiful and are a gift to everyone in your life.

Day 28—Review Day

1. What do you understand about the five stages of grief?
2. Do you recognize them within your own healing through life?
3. Did you feel any changes or shifts in energy when meditating this week?
4. Please submit your eulogy.
5. What were the most common words that were given to you by friends?

WELCOME TO WEEK *five*

This week we are going to explore the vital connection with your guides that you need within Mediumship. Any mediums that you watch or go for a reading with have a strong connection to their guides. As the name suggests, the Spirit Guide will guide you and be your companions throughout life, and will help protect you when times get hard and save you from tragic situations. Therefore everyone can benefit from having a relationship with their guide. We all have the gift of having a guide, so we just need to believe.

Hopefully by now you are starting to believe in the connection that you have. You have started to change your life, habits of "escaping" into media, and other sources. All aspects of drama have reduced considerably. The connection to self is also going to help you build that strong relationship with your guide and allow you to connect fully to the world of Spirit. The signs are around you, and you are now seeing them much more clearly.

Having worked as a medium for over twenty years, I cannot stress how important it is to have this relationship, and you must start to embrace your guide as someone you would love in your life. Your guide needs to be your best friend, companion, and confidant.

Let me explain how I work with my guide.

If I struggle with the connection directly with the Spirit, I will call upon my guide to help me make that communication stronger. The guide will connect with the Spirit and relay the message to me directly. The disconnect with Spirit could happen for many reasons—one of them may be because I am not feeling well or my connection isn't strong for whatever reason—however, my connection to my guide is *always* strong.

The only way I can explain how my guide is when "he" works with me is that we are *one*. It's like there is no separation: I connect to my soul and he connects to my soul also, so we are soul connected and then I can explore the communication.

My guide's name is Ben. He has been with me all my life, but I have only been consciously aware of him for the last fifteen years.

Over this week you will have daily exercises to connect with your guides, and they will help you with your connection to Spirit. I believe, after having studied Mediumship for years, that you need to establish your connection to your guide before you start to work on your senses, which is what is going to come next week. The reason is you are still working with your senses, but your guides will enable you to highly develop your senses further.

Day 29

You may already feel a connection with your guides but you can never have too much communication with them. Once you establish a firm and strong bond with them, you can call upon them at any time to help you with your work and life. However, first we must understand angels.

We are not going to be covering angels in depth in this book;

I am not an expert but there are many out there who are. If you feel that this is something that you would like to pursue, then I can recommend many workshops and books from people who very much deal with the angelic realm.

What I will share with you is that it took me a long time to believe in this. The reason why I am telling you this is that I feel you need to know that it's OK to be skeptical. It's actually very common. I know a yoga instructor who is incredibly connected to his soul and intuition but does not believe in what I do, so it's not a problem if you have an air of skepticism about you.

However, let me share with you what made me believe. I had been giving readings for a number of years and had moved from my home into an office environment since I was giving about twenty-five readings a week. Many people had been mentioning angels and their connection to them, but I just wasn't sure. I sat on the fence with splinters digging into me....

But something made me question it.... I bought some angel cards and started to play with them to see if they really worked. I started to realize that every question I asked, the answer that each card that I chose was relevant. I was quite taken aback by it but then the element of doubt came in again.

There were several incidences that happened all within a short space of time. Over that time I started to believe. And as they say, there are no coincidences.

The doubt about angels resurfaced again, and when that happened something came along to reinforce it....

I was giving platform readings one night at my local Spiritual Church and out of the lights in the ceiling a shadow was created... but it wasn't a shadow really; it formed a bright-white angel shape. My eyes, I thought, were playing tricks on me, but I had to embrace it and say that there was an angel there. Others saw it too.

Then finally I was giving a reading and the lady's husband said, "I am with the angels." She started to cry and of course I was sympathetic to her grief but inside I was thinking "…angels…yeah, yeah, really?"

Next thing I knew a single angel feather floated down between my client and me… I was amazed. That was it…I was a total believer.

There had been too many things that had happened over a short period of time for me not to believe.

I never doubted it again, and that was a number of years ago, and I still ask the angels for protection and help now.

So like I said, I have had many angel experiences over my time working as a medium, but it's not my area of expertise.

Today's Exercise

Sit within you sacred space and, in your journal, write down your opinion of Spirit Guides and helpers in the afterlife. Why do you feel that you have them and who might they be for you? Do you believe that they are family members or that you do not know them?

I will give you more information about Spirit Guides, but you must have your own opinion on guides before you believe.

Next you are going to do this guided mediation so that you can start your connection to your guides. You are going to get to know your guides and ask them questions.

I recommend that you start with yes or no questions. But each question should be very simple and only asked once. If you don't get an answer, move on to the next question. You may be working with telepathic thoughts to communicate with your guides, but make sure all your senses are open and ready to receive any information.

You may get:

- A pressure on top of your head—this is the opening of the Crown Chakra.

- A sensation on the left side of the body or face—this is the right side of the brain, the intuitive side, opening.

- The voice that you hear may sound the similar to your own, but it will be a tone higher or lower than yours.

Ensure that you are not going to be disturbed. Listen to your thoughts only and allow the answers to come naturally.

Day 30

We all have a Spirit Guide; in fact most of us have more than one. The average number of guides is five, usually a mix of male and female. I always refer to them as my "team" of helpers.

They will be a mixture of:

- spiritual guardians

- healers

- individuals with past life connections to you, deceased relatives, or close friends

Many people go through life not realizing that they have someone on their side who is there for their own good or to help guide them through life. Our guides have many roles that they play, but their main job is to teach us spiritual truth. The guides are our helpers.

Your connection to your Spirit Guides is one of the most essential parts of your development. Not only will they help you with your life and fulfilling your life contract, but they are also your direct connection to Spirit.

You may have had connections to your guides before this book. This section is only going to strengthen this. If you have not had a connection to your guides, then it will help open up the lines of communication.

Life Contract

 Before we do go further, we need to understand what a "life contract" is. This is a contract that was set by you and your guides. This is your incarnation that was predestined before you were even born. However, you still have free will to make choices and decisions that aren't in your contract. To understand what seems to be a contradiction—predestination and free will—follow me through an imaginary scenario.

Imagine that you're out running errands, and you drop off a prescription at the pharmacy. In the time it takes for the prescription to be filled, you decide to do some shopping. As you're coming out of a store, about to head back to the pharmacy, you run into an old friend whom you haven't seen for a while. The two of you decide to get some coffee and catch up on each other's lives. Ultimately, the predestined plan is to pick up your prescription—but by virtue of your free will, you altered that plan when you chose to go have coffee with your old friend.

Some may question if the meeting with your friend was actually free will or if it was meant to happen—in other words, predestination. But whether your friend was part of the plan or not doesn't matter since you always have a choice to do something different.

Think of it this way: collecting your prescription is the part that's predestined, but when and how you decide to collect it is up to you. This is similar to the contract you made in the afterlife, which requires many things to be accomplished—but there will always be tests along the way, and you'll forever be making choices thanks to your free will.

We are all on a journey that we have decided upon. This is the same for everyone on the earth plane. So when you have clients who blame everything else and everyone else in the universe for their lives, you have to remind them of this. It's not easy but often by using the analogy that I use, people tend to understand it. It may take a period of time for it to sink in, but trust me, it will.

The main job of our guides is to keep us on track so that we can complete our life contract. These guides have been with you all of your life and, believe me, they want to communicate with you. This will not happen until you open yourself up to them. Your guides love you very much, and they will do anything within their power to help you and protect you. Meeting, getting to know, and learning to trust your guides is the next step that you must take on this spiritual journey.

When we sleep, we connect with our guides. We discuss many things such as whether we are on the right pathway or not and if it should change. Within this time, we can decide what is best for our souls. So we do have control even though we may not realize it on a conscious level.

Today's Exercise

Think about your life and how there have been many things that could have "tested" you. I would like you to write down some of those things in your journal and write about how your guide may have actually helped you, and what you learned from this incident.

I would also like you to think about your life and the journey that you are currently on. I'm not just talking about studying mediumship; I'm talking about everything in life. Write down some of the questions that you would love to have answered about your life.

Write down some of the things that you would like to change, why they should be changed, and what they would bring to your life in a spiritual capacity.

During your meditation, you are going to find out more about your guides. This is an opportunity for you to really discover more about your guides.

Questions to ask when you encounter a guide:

- Are you my guide?
- Are you my master guide?
- Will you help me with the spiritual work that I am embarking on?
- Will you help me with my pathway through life?
- Have we had a past life together?
- Are you someone I knew in this life?
- Are you going to help me?
- Are there any more guides that you are going to introduce to me?
- What is your name?
- Can you give me the first initial?

Make sure that you record your results in your journal.

Day 31

We are now going to explore the hierarchy of the Spirit Realm. It's actually quite incredible when you know how the levels all work with each other to help you make the most of your life and fulfill your life path.

There has been a lot of talk about ascended masters over recent years, but that is only because Spirituality has finally come out of the closet where it has been hidden for decades. Ascended masters have actually been around for centuries. While it's important to understand the hierarchy of the Spirit Realm we are not going to delve deeply into these masters. There are plenty of websites with information about these masters and their teachings. You may also find conflicting views on them. So you have to decide your own beliefs.

What I will share with you is that these masters have walked on the earth plane and know the life lessons that we all encounter. During their time they completed their life contracts and balanced karma in many ways. Many people suggest that they are god-like or that the masters are a collective energy that we refer to as "god." No matter what, they act as teachers of Spirituality to everyone who is earth bound. There are many ascended masters, and Jesus is said to be one of the masters.

When I was introduced to my elder, who is not an ascended master but a soul who is higher than a Master Guide, which is explained in detail in the next section, he shared with me a piece of information about god, who is believed to be the collective energies of the ascended masters. I will share it with you now.

There is a place in the afterlife where only the elders are allowed, and then only by special invitation. It is called the Kingdom of Power, and it is where the Highest Master resides, whom some refer to as God.

The Kingdom is always visible in the distance, surrounded by rainbows and connected by a golden bridge that spans a great distance. The celestial beings live there—the angels and all those who accompany the Almighty, whom you call God. But souls cannot just walk up to this place and knock on the door. Many try but never make it. Imagine walking and walking but never getting to your destination. No matter how far you go, your destination is always the same distance away...it is as if you are on a treadmill and never getting anywhere!

The Kingdom is a place of exquisite peace and harmony, and a meeting with God is an enlightening and beautiful experience. There is a hierarchy in the Kingdom, but it is not driven by ego. God is a higher force that governs all higher senses—such as nature, beauty, the planets, healing, comfort, and people and their growth. God governs everything, but he cannot control everything, so he sends helpers to oversee the many domains of existence. He passes on many tasks to the elders, who pass them on to the Spirit Guides, who then pass them on to the living.

You can see how we are all trying to achieve God's purpose! It is about teamwork. No religion, no fighting, no hassles to divide souls.... And he wants everyone to live in harmony.

As you might imagine, it is a difficult job that God has at the moment. But things are going to change for the better, and then there will be more of a semblance of peace in the world. This may take centuries to unfold, but eventually it will come to pass.

The Elders

I wrote about the elders in *Survival of the Soul,* when I was first introduced to them. An elder is a guiding Spirit who holds your life contract. My elder is called Josiah and, when I was introduced to him, he told me that the term elder was only a label and that he didn't consider himself to be of a higher status than any other soul. Josiah made it clear that he still has growth and learning to accomplish—as all do in the afterlife—but he is a highly evolved spirit who has chosen to take on this role.

Your life contract contains the lessons that you committed yourself to learning during your time on the earth plane. We all have such a contract: an agreement we drew up with the help of our elder and Spirit Guides to record and confirm the lessons we will be learning.

If a life contract doesn't call for a specific arrangement, then returning souls will seek advice from their elders about who should guide them. The elders will then prepare the chosen guides to ensure that those souls are taken through their lives correctly and maintain their paths.

As you know, an elder is a highly evolved soul whose purpose is to enlighten you and help you on your journey. Your elder is yours throughout eternity even if your elder may decide to incarnate again. You will always be connected and will never break your bond. Yet once a soul becomes evolved enough to become an elder, the soul is usually content to stay and help others. It's rare that an elder will see a reason to return to Earth, unless it's been requested of the elder through a higher source.

It's important to know that elders have all walked the earth plane before, so they know the lessons that humans have to learn, as well as the trials and tribulations experienced in this dimension. They have lived many lives, in fact, some harder than others. They've experienced everything you can imagine—including poverty, wealth, abuse, greed, love, illness, and many other situations. They've gone through all of these challenges so that they truly know how to help souls preparing to become human.

People on Earth often question why their lives are so difficult, but rarely do they consider that their hardships may be there for a reason. I've been guilty of this on many occasions, and I've finally come to believe that human beings have difficult lives because we're all being groomed for a higher purpose. (The fact that even elders have experienced tough times especially proves my point.) This is something that you will also have to share with your clients.

Master Guide

Our life contract and the journey that we have planned is something we all hold within us. It's kept in our soul; we have it hidden deep within our awareness.

The life that we had between lives was a journey of learning, healing, and discovery, and during that time we decided what our pathway was going to be in this life. We decided the people that we would meet, the parents we would have, and the situations that we would find ourselves in.

We planned every part of our lives, and we knew all the emotions that we were going to experience. We knew all of this but we also didn't do it alone, we had a master guide by our side as we planned the life that we were about to take.

The master guide is a soul who has had many incarnations on the earth plane and has learned many spiritual lessons. You will have had many of those incarnations on the earth plane together, and the two of you would have been in many situations and circumstances. You may have been lovers, friends, brothers, sisters, family...the list goes on and on. Both of you would have been both sexes too. So you have experienced many things together. You made a pact that you help each other as you journey through life, guiding each other in different lives. These are some of the things we can find out when we talk to our master guides later and build new relationships with them.

At some point your master guides would have decided that that was the route they were going to take, and then they would have started to prepare for their new roles by being general guides, which we will discuss shortly. They have spent much time in Spirit and so they have become highly developed in spiritual ways. They chose to remain close to the earth life and act as a link and teacher.

It's a great honor to be asked to guide a soul since it's an acknowledgment that you have evolved and can be trusted to take another through life's lessons.

You chose them to help guide you through life, based on the spiritual lessons that you plan to learn in your lives.

Your master guide will then take you through everything—your life, your birth, your parents—and will stay with you until you transition back into the afterlife.

So with this in mind, your master guide cannot be someone you knew physically in this lifetime.

However, our master guides will bring in other guides who can help you throughout your life. These guides may be people you have known.

My grandmother was the first guide or helper I was aware of, but she could only take me to a certain level. Once I achieved that level, she introduced me to the guide I have worked with for some time, Ben. Slowly I have met other guides, and they have worked with me on different levels. I now realize that Ben is my master guide.

Our master guides will not make decisions for us; they will only act as a service to us if we ask for them. Of course they will step in and intervene but just know that they will not make decisions for us.

Today's Exercise

I would like you create a space in which it is safe for your guides to visit you. This could be your sacred space, but it needs to be somewhere safe where you will not be disturbed when you honor them.

You may wish to have an offering or something like that, but you are now going to welcome your master guide, if possible.

You are just going to connect to yourself through gentle meditation and breath work, and you are going to write everything and anything that you need too. You are going to ask for your guides to connect and speak through your writing. You will be amazed at what happens.

Day 32

Today it's important for you to understand that there are other guides around you who want to help you through your life, and that you may know some of them.

We all have other guides who pop in and out who help us with our work and journey through life. Even though Spirits are energy, our guides present themselves as physical people. They come through with a sense of humor.

Master guides gather a team they believe will help us throughout life. Each guide will help you for a certain period of time in your life depending on circumstance, and then move on. Let me explain: guides each have their own jobs; think of them as teachers in a school where they all have specialized subjects.

For instance, when you have relationship difficulties, there will be a guide that will help you specifically in this area. With career opportunities, there will be another guide, and so on and so forth.

We can go through a whole host of guides throughout our lives. Some will only work with you once, while some will be back many times. It's the job of your master guide to determine this.

However, we connect with our guides constantly. Most people connect with their guides in their sleep, but for those who are on the spiritual path can connect with them at any time of the day or night. We will practice this communication this week.

While your guides are with you, their job is to teach you certain things in life, often spiritual lessons that help you grow.

It's essential to build relationships and trust with your guides.

However, what you must realize is that your guide will only appear when you are ready. If you are not ready to meet, you won't. Remember your guide knows what is right for you. Just because you haven't met your guide doesn't mean that you can't connect to the afterlife, because you can. I did for about two years before I met Ben, and it then changed my life!

It took me a while to realize that my grandmother was the first Spirit I felt guiding me. I thought that she was always going to be the one working with me, but I was mistaken. However, looking back, I was so thankful that it was her to start with. Something very bizarre happened one night, and my grandmother helped me through it. That was the night I was introduced to Ben, my master guide, who has helped me progress my knowledge further.

It happened one Sunday night while I was lying in bed. I didn't ask to be introduced to my guide; I was simply trying to get to sleep. However, my grandmother came to me, and she looked about thirty years younger than she did when she passed over. She walked down one side of the bed and then up the other side. But as she came up the other side she was joined by a man who stood at the foot of the bed. He looked Italian and dressed in black. He had longish wavy dark hair and beautiful eyes…I couldn't take me eyes off him; I was mesmerized. She said, "This is your guide now. I have taken you as far as I can. It's his job now. His name is Ben."

I was, as you can imagine, a little shocked and slightly scared. Even though I work with Spirit all the time, it still can be a little unnerving when they appear unexpectedly. Even more so since he looked like he was alive!

From that moment onward, he has been with me, and we have built up an amazing relationship, and it's one I value and respect. I couldn't do my work without him.

I realized that my grandmother was the one who was guiding me for a while to get me used to the work that I had to do and to introduce me to my master guide. She still pops in and out, but normally she only comes when I have something that is difficult to share with someone else.

Today's Exercise

Prepare for your meditation in the same way you have in the past. By now you should feel comfortable with your guide. Here are some personal spiritual questions that you may wish to ask:

- Are you my only Spirit Guide?

- How many do I have?

- I would like to meet another guide today. May another guide come to talk with me?

- What is your name?

- Do you work with (name of first guide)?
- What is your function in my life? (This can be asked of both guides.)
- Am I on the right spiritual path?
- Will you guide me to the next part of my Spirit journey?

There are many questions that you may wish to ask. But make sure that you have them prepared before this meditation. Take notes and record as much as you can; you will find this part fascinating.

Day 33

The communication you will have with your master guides is something that is incredibly sacred. They will share with you so many things about your life, and you will find that once you have opened the communication that it will never stop. There will be times that you don't feel your master guide as strongly because one of your other guides has had to come forward to help you through a situation, but your master guide will always be there in the background, ensuring that things are working perfectly for you.

How you communicate with your guides is something that is going to be very personal to you. I cannot tell you a right or a wrong way, because there isn't one. It's something that you will discover on your own, and you will find that they will not always communicate in the same way. You may have one way for your master guide and another way for the general guides.

Sometimes they will be the little voice you hear in your head—your thoughts. Oftentimes they speak to you in a dream state (daydream), meditation, an altered state of consciousness, through certain things that occur in your life, or through art, music, dance, or acting. If they really want to make a point they will drop something on you, like a book, as if to say, "pay attention!"

As you start to work more with your clairaudience, you will start to hear your guides. It's then that you will find that you can have open dialogue with them, and the more you do this the more your clairaudience will open up. Of course they will show you images as well, but often it will be easier to hear your guides.

You will also start to pick up on the differences of energy and be able to understand when it's one of your guides and when it's Spirit.

Spirit Guides travel with us. They travel with us at night when we sleep. This is the time that they teach us. They cannot manifest a physical form, as they are pure energy, but they will present you with a likeness of themselves as best they can.

Today's Exercise

Sit quietly, relax your mind, and ask your guides to give you a sign to show you they are there, working with you. You may find that you have just one sign or you may have a sign per guide that comes to assist you. When you ask for this sign, state that it is to be something you will recognize and that's specific to them.

Don't tell them what it needs to be; they will decide for you. It may take a day or two to receive that sign but you will get it. It could be a piece of music, a chime, something to do with nature...there are many things it could be but this will help you to determine that it's your guide who is working with you.

Day 34

I know what it's like to be busy; in fact it's something I thrive on. Many people are like this but having time to yourself is essential, and while you are cutting out the media over the next few weeks, you will have time to focus on connecting with Spirit. However, lives get back to normal and, as it gets busier and busier, you may find that your connection to Spirit outside of giving readings will become less and less. Please don't feel guilty about it…it's normal.

However, there will be times when you forget about your Spirit Guide and you will struggle with things in your life. You will feel like you are struggling alone when actually your master guide or another guide is screaming at you to say, "Hey, I'm here to talk to you. I can give you the answers!" It happened to me. Now if I have a situation that I need some clarity on, I will wait until the "chatter" in my mind has stopped (that is *very* important because otherwise you will not be able to hear clearly), and then I open the communication with Ben or someone else.

Let me explain. When we are upset, our minds fill with chatter. We need to take ourselves away from the chatter, so that may mean that we have to distance ourselves from a situation or person. You have to become centered to allow the chatter to come and go. Do your breathing exercises and, if it helps you, your physical exercises. Ground yourself. It may take you ten minutes to do this, or it may take you an hour…however long it takes you just take the time to do it.

Then, open the lines of communication with your guides. I am going to help you with opening the lines of communication with them in a moment, but here is a suggestion that it will help you: When you are in a space that you feel is right to communicate and you are not listening to your own chatter, ask your Spirit Guides if now is the right time to communicate with them. You will feel, know, or hear a yes or a no.

If you get a yes, you can ask them about the situation that just occurred, but I want you to remain calm and relaxed when you ask the questions and to *listen* to the answers. There is no point in asking the questions if you are not going to listen to the answers that are given to you. You may not like what you hear, but it's the truth of the situation.

When you become really clear with your guides, they will share some amazing things with you. I remember having an argument with someone. I called upon Ben, and he said, "Well, I am working with A.M, and she tells me that this is how the other person is feeling, however, this is what you should do to handle the situation" (A.M is the abbreviated name for the Spirit Guide of the other person). So what I realized was that I was being given the name of the other person's guide—which was incredible (as normally this is personal information that only you can find out)—learning how the other person felt in that situation, and also how to handle it. I was amazed, I followed what I was told, and it all worked out perfectly.

Our guides will work with other people's guides to make the best of situations.

You will see that establishing strong links with your guides will help you in many situations, not only during Mediumship communication. But you will have to learn to communicate with them on the go, and this is easy. You just have to speak to them and address your questions or thoughts to them. They will hear you and help you in a way that you will hear and understand.

For example, as you go about your day you will encounter a decision you will have to make such as "What should I eat for dinner?" Ask the question in your mind, even if you are in transit, and you will get an answer.

Many people, myself included, love to talk to Spirit when they are driving. You may find that you are not exactly focused on the road, though! You must pay attention to your driving, but you can ask questions.

Think your question. Listen to your thoughts. You will get your answer!

The more you communicate, the better the relationship you build.

Today's Exercise

I would like you to connect with yourself and start to talk to yourself and ask questions. This is something that you need to do all day. Ask questions and listen to the answers that you receive.

When you are able to "listen" to your own thoughts and be aware of your own feelings, then you will be able to connect to your guides.

Start to ask questions and be aware of how you get the answers. Some would say that it's your higher self but actually it's your Spirit Guide who will be guiding you.

Hold this connection all day, if you can, and constantly talk to yourself and ask questions and see what answers you get.

Just be in constant communication. At the end of the day, record any interesting information or what you learned by listening to your guides.

Establish a strong relationship with them. Even though I have been working and communicating with Ben for a long time, I still do these exercises to ensure that I maintain a connection. When I feel the energy change and a new guide step in then I repeat all the exercises again so that I can get to know my guides more.

Day 35—Review Day

1. Please describe your connection to your guides this week. Describe any interesting information about who they are and if you have had past lives together.

2. Please explain what you understand about the hierarchy of Spirit Guides.

3. What do you believe a life path or life contract is?

4. Do you feel that you have made a strong connection with your guide?

5. Would you like to pursue this connection?

WELCOME TO WEEK *Six*

This week we are going to start to hone our senses and explore how Spirit communicates with us. One thing I must say is that *we* make it difficult: we constantly question what we are getting and how it's coming to us. So it's time to stop questioning and just allow the information to flow. Let me explain. If I ask someone who lives in America what they would put with two slices of bread and some bacon, there would be no hesitation, and they would say lettuce, tomato, and mayonnaise. If I asked the same question of someone who lived in England, they would not hesitate in saying tomato ketchup or HP Sauce. If I told those who were bought up in America what the English said, their response would be "ewwwww disgusting."

So this proves my point. We have been conditioned to think and believe things in a certain way so that we have an understanding of what is right and wrong. This causes us to think too much into the information that we are getting and, because we think it's wrong, we don't say it. It's a classic case of what happens when mediums uses their heads and "think" too much.

So it's time to stop thinking and go beyond the perception of right and wrong and go into ultimate surrender, into a playground of the knowledge that we can gain. When we surrender to that place, you can't even imagine what happens. We get information and messages galore, but getting to that place is something that can be hard for many, myself included.

When I used to get names during reading, I would think "No, I'm wrong. That can't be it," so I wouldn't say it. Next thing I would hear my client mention the Spirit's name, and I would kick myself for not saying it. Now I just say it, and I don't worry about whether I am wrong or not. I am getting it for a reason and somewhere the information will fit and make sense. I don't "try" to make it fit...it is what it is.

That is the secret.

So over the next two weeks you need to let go and say what you get, and don't "think" about what you are getting. You will be working on developing your senses to receive information.

This is called Mental Mediumship. We are going to receive information by using our psychic senses and by working through the senses that we already have. There is another type of Mediumship, which is called Physical Mediumship, where we look for physical things to prove that life continues. However, the most rewarding side of Mediumship is when you can deliver a message fully in the Mental Mediumship.

We have five senses in our physical body, which is how we receive information daily. It's how we communicate and survive in this physical world. These senses keep us alive and out of danger. They are sight, hearing, touch, taste, and smell.

However, there is another sense that we also utilize but that some people don't believe that we have...

Knowing

There are times when we just "know" something. Some would call it intuition; whatever label you decide to use, it's actually a sense that we use all the time yet doubt that we have. We know when the phone is going to ring and who it is before looking at the caller ID. It's quite incredible when we think about it.

When we gather information from Spirit we use all of these senses, but the primary ones are sight, hearing, touch, and knowing.

That is not to say that we don't receive information through taste and smell, because we do. We will often smell someone's perfume or cigar smoke or we will taste coffee when we are alone and there is no reason to be experiencing this. Well, Spirit are giving you a strong smell or taste just to show you that they are there. This is really the beginning stage of opening your awareness, so do not neglect these experiences, because they are powerful. However, in the Mediumship world, it really doesn't give you much information. So we are going to work on developing the other senses so that you can really enhance the experience of receiving a message from Spirit.

Day 36

Within Mental Mediumship you have two types of knowing.

- control

- perception

Control is when you allow the Spirit to take some form of control over your body, such as Trance Mediumship. I must stress that the Spirit will never take you over entirely, and it's extremely hard to become "possessed," so please do not worry.

Perception Mediumship is the most common way for anyone to connect with Spirit.

The main purpose of Mediumship is to provide evidence that the soul continues to live on and survives the process of "death." We all know that this is the case or you wouldn't be where you are now on this spiritual journey.

We are going to focus on our senses.

Before you go further, you need to determine which is your predominant sense. You will say that all of them are equal—it may seem that way—but I can guarantee that there will be one sense that is stronger than the others.

Today's Exercise

I would like you to think about the language you use and how you react to people around you.

When people tell you something that you can relate to, how do you respond to them? This is often a good indication of your dominant sense.

"I see what you are saying."

"I hear what you are saying."

"I know how you feel."

"I feel for you."

Even though this is a simple exercise, you will be able to tell what your predominant sense is. This is something that you will need to be aware of as you move forward as you connect to Spirit

- **Visual**—seeing. "I see what you are saying," or "I see what you mean." If you think that this may relate to you, you may find that you receive your information via clairvoyance, which means "clear seeing."

- **Auditory**—hearing. "I hear what you are saying." If you think that this may relate to you, you may find that you receive your information via clairaudient, which means "clear hearing."

- **Kinesthetic**—feeling. "I feel for you." If you think that this may relate to you, you may find that you receive your information via clairsentient, which means "clear sensing."

- **Knowing**—sense of knowing. "I know what you are going through." If you think that this may relate to you, you may find that you get your information through claircognizance, which means "clear knowing."

You may find that you are one or two of these, and if this is the case, then these are your primary senses. Throughout the rest of the day watch how you work with your primary senses during everything you do.

Day 37

When our loved ones pass away, the first thing we do is look for the signs that they are around us. We look at everything, wondering and questioning if that is that our loved one. It's a constant thing that goes through our heads. We see roses and wonder if those are them. We see birds and wonder if those are them. We see and question it all. It's extremely normal and not something you should think is silly because *everyone* does it, including myself.

This is part of developing our clairvoyance. We want to "see" our loved ones, but in reality, do we?

If you saw your loved ones suddenly standing in front of you, you would freak out. And let me explain why.

Your conscious mind knows that they have passed over. You are living a life where their physical presence no longer exists in this world so your conscious brain will go into a state of shock knowing that it's wrong, and there will be an immediate sense of panic.

Spirit may manifest this way but you will find that if they do, it will only be for a split second, and in that period of time your conscious mind will go into panic, and Spirit of your loved ones will be gone since it takes too much energy to maintain that state with them.

A Spirit, as we know, doesn't have a body; the body decays and leaves the physical earth plane when it's no longer needed. Yet while the body is alive and living the physical life that we are leading now, our soul is attached to the body by what is called a silver cord. Every night when we sleep, we leave our bodies and travel. Some of us remember it and others don't, but while we are traveling far and wide, we don't lose the connection to our physical bodies since they are still connected by the silver cords. The cord is energetically flexible and allows the movement of the soul within the body. It will bring the soul back to the body when it's needed.

However, the silver cord breaks when the process of death has started. The soul then leaves the body at a twenty- to thirty-degree angle, not by floating up. It floats across.

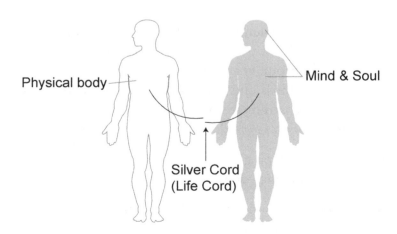

Physical body

Mind & Soul

Silver Cord
(Life Cord)

Every living thing has a vibration, a frequency that it resonates with. One the earth plane we are extremely dense and our vibration is low, but when we are in the afterlife our we have release the physical dense vibrational energy and are now Spirit and our vibration is suddenly greater than anything you can imagine. Every sound is magnified, every vision is brighter, and the love is so immense as you transcend the white light into the afterlife where your family and friends greet you.

The afterlife and the Earthplane coexist within the same universe. There is no heaven or hell. It's something I discussed and explored greatly in *Survival of the Soul*. For me and many others who have had a near death experience, have all said it's an incredible experience.

People often ask me that "if the experience is so incredible, then why do they want to come back and visit us?" Well it's a very good question, so let me ask you this: when you go away on vacation and you arrive at your destination, what is one of the first things that you do? When I asked my many students and fans this question, they replied that they checked in with family and friends to let them know that they had arrived safely.

Well that is exactly what Spirit does: they check in to let us know that they have arrived. They can't do it physically as they don't have a body, but they do it by leaving signs. Because they are still quite grounded on the earth plane, they find it easy to give us quick glimpses of them, and also to dream with us. As they become more and more stable in the afterlife, they are no longer felt so frequently in the earth plane. This is why we often question why they are not visiting us now.

Well, it could be for two reasons:

1. Because we have gotten so used to their energy that we no longer "feel" when they are around.
2. Because they know that we are getting used to a life without them. They are still with us, but only when we need them.

Your loved ones will never leave you, they are always around you.

So it's important for us to look for the signs and take the signs that we get as messages that they are still around us.

The secret to spotting signs is that when you see something and wonder "Is it a sign?" you can guarantee that it is!

Today's Exercise

Sit in your sacred space and meditate for a little while just to get yourself into that space of peace and relaxation.

Ask for your loved ones to come close and give you a sign that they are around you.

When you come out of meditation, the first thing that you see, hear, or notice is normally your sign. Ask them to show you the signs throughout the day.

As you go about your day, look for these signs that your loved ones are around you. The signs may change but they will be there.

Here is a list of signs that you may wish to look for. Remember that they can come through various ways.

Vision	Hearing
• Angel feathers	• Voice in your head
• Coins on the floor	• Music
• Seeing people who remind you of your loved one	• Words
	• Static interference
• Seeing their favorite things	• Whispers
• Dreams/daydreams	• Bells ringing

Nature
- Wind
- Butterflies
- Dragonflies
- Flies
- Birds
- Hummingbirds
- Rainbows
- Flowers

Shapes
- Cloud formations
- Stars
- Shapes in fabric
- Orbs in photos
- Numbers

Energy & Technology
- Seeing sparkles out of the corners of your eyes
- Flickering lights
- Flickering of the TV
- Blank e-mails
- Phone ringing and no one is there

Physical
- Pictures/items moving
- Light breeze
- Temperature changes
- "Knowing" that they are with you

As well as signs, we also get numbers that repeat. Doreen Virtue's wonderful book *Angel Numbers 101 (copyright 2008)* can help you understand them, but here is an overview.

Numbers

111 – The universe has taken note of your thoughts, which will be manifesting.

222 – New ideas are about to grow into reality. Don't give up!

333 – Ascended masters are with you.

444 – Angels are close by helping you.

555 – Change is about to happen.

666 – Your thoughts are out of balance, and you are too busy in the material world. Focus on spirituality.

777 – Keep up the good work. You are being praised!

888 – A phase of your life is about to end. New beginnings

999 – End of an era with your personal life or, if you are a healer, you are being called to help the universe.

Day 38

Yesterday you started to be aware of your clairvoyance by looking for signs that your loved ones are around you. These signs are very much part of your development, and the more you see them, the more you will develop. Not only do we see the signs, but we also

get visions in our dreams. Our dreams are incredible because when we sleep we actually come out of our bodies and raise our vibrations, making it so we can connect with our loved ones. This is something that is powerful. We raise our vibrations and Spirit lowers their vibrations and we meet somewhere in the middle.

Sometimes our dreams get twisted, and we don't always see our loved ones in good places, or they are not talking to us for whatever reason. I want to assure you that they are not in a bad place. It's our own mind that creates this.

Remember back to when I was talking about how we want to see our loved ones but our conscious minds know that it's not real, and we start to panic? Well the same thing happens in our dreams. In our dream-like state, the conscious mind remains active. And when we raise our vibrations and meet our loved ones, our conscious minds say, "no, that's wrong," and it gets all twisted up. That's why we have the dreams that we have.

You will find that the more you meditate and accept the afterlife into your life as a "normal" thing that dreams like this will become less frequent.

Throughout this week and the rest of this book you are going to keep a dream journal, this should be different from your original journal and document any dreams that you have. No matter what they are about, if you remember the dream, then write it down. When we dream, we access the knowledge that we need through life. We connect with our souls and are given information that we need. So no matter what you dream, write it down.

If you find that you are dreaming and start to wake up, stay still, keep your eyes closed, and let your dream play out without any influence. It'll be amazing what you discover.

Another way to open our clairvoyance is by using our imagination.

Let's think back to when we were children, and we allowed our imaginations to run away with us. We could create anything in our minds. Remember what we did with cardboard boxes? When we were a child they were the best things ever. We were kings, queens, and action heroes, and we always saved the day. These games kept our minds active, and we used the creative side of the brain. This is the side that we use to open our awareness to the afterlife.

So the more imaginative we can be, the better. You will often find that artists, dancers, singers, and just about anyone who has a creative flare will be in touch with their intuitive or mediumistic side.

Today's Exercise

Start your dream journal and keep it by the side of your bed for the remainder of this book. Anytime you have a dream and remember it, write it down. If you find that you are dreaming in the middle of the night and need to get up, just write key words that will remind you in the morning of what you dreamed about.

In addition, you need to write a fairy tale. It can be as elaborate as you like but it must start with "Once upon a time…" and end with "and they all lived happily ever after."

Let your mind run free.

Enjoy!

Day 39

Now we are going to work on our claircognizance, as it tends to work hand in hand with clairvoyance. This sense is one of the easiest to develop, but many people, especially those who overanalyze things, will want to know "*Why* do I just know these things?" Well my answer to that is "Why do you want to know why? Just stop questioning and let it be!"

If you have an analytical brain, you are going to be very good at claircognizance. However you won't know why you know certain things.

Claircognizance is the sense of knowing. There are times when we have all said, "I just know I'm right," and we are.

Tony Stockwell will often say something like "I know that your mother is in Spirit, and I know she had a tumor on her right lung." He has an excellent sense of claircognizance, but he also intertwines it with his other senses. It's incredible to watch him work.

To be in touch with our claircognizance, we have to be connected to our souls. When we connect with our souls, it's like joining the underground network of souls. We pick up information that way. Therefore, we just know information about Spirits and people that we are not supposed to know in our conscious mind.

We can do this for ourselves when we want to gain access to information about ourselves, and so we connect with our souls and the life path. But when we want to find out more information about others, we need to really connect to self and then expand that connection out beyond what we know.

Automatic writing is an excellent way to develop claircognizance. You just need to write without thinking or receiving (hearing) information. It's just writing random words or sentences that may or may not make sense.

It's always good to work with a pen and paper and to write since it keeps the flow of energy going. If you stop, it will block your energy.

...

Today's Exercise

For the remainder of this week you are going to sit in your sacred space with your journal and pen and write. Write anything that comes to you. You are not going to control what you are writing; you are just going to write.

Don't think!

Allow your hand to flow across the page. If you wish, before you start, you can set an intention and ask your Spirit Guides and loved ones to step forward and give you a message for the day.

Remember to do this daily.

Day 40

Claircognizance is something that I work with a great deal. You will find that the more you develop it, the more it will become second nature to you, especially if you feel that working as a medium is your calling in life.

When you connect to Spirit, you will find that you will just know some things about them, such as:

- relationship to the client
- male or female
- age (young/old)
- how the Spirit passed
- more intricate details about the passing, for example murder/ suicide
- personality
- know the feelings of the Spirit without feeling them

You can also use a pendulum to help you with this, just to make sure that you are right. This works by using your own natural energy and what you "know." You will find that, once you work with a pendulum, you will love it. A pendulum is a long piece of string with a weight hanging from it. You can get fancy ones with crystals, although a necklace with a pendant works equally well.

To start, keep your hand still, and ask the pendulum to show you the direction it's going to swing for a yes. Then asks the pendulum for the direction of no. The pendulum should swing in two different ways.

Now you can start to ask questions. Start by asking questions that you know, such as "Is my name (your name)?" You will find that the pendulum will swing in the way that represents the truth.

Continue to practice with this until you feel confident that it's working for you, and then you can use it to work with Spirit.

Today's Exercise

Practice working with your pendulum, and then sit in your sacred space and ask Spirit to come forward. When you feel the energy connecting with you, write down what you know to be correct—whether the Spirit is male or female, old or young—and continue until you have built a picture of what you believe is correct. Now double check it with your pendulum.

Ask the pendulum the questions to see if your answers are correct.

Today you are also going to practice a reading.

We are going to work with friends or family members, and we are going to ask them to think of a person that they would like to connect with, and then we will share what we are getting from our claircognizance and clairvoyance. Then we can also work with our pendulums to clarify things.

Please be aware that just because people want their dads, doesn't mean that you will get them…. Just say everything that you get and *do not worry* about being wrong…it happens. Practice makes perfect. If you find that you are not getting anywhere, then ask your friend who to connect with and see if you can pick up that soul's personality and traits.

You can then back everything up with the pendulum.

Have Fun!

Day 41

This week we have been working with our clairvoyance and claircognizance, and now it's time to bring it all together.

Today's Exercise

For the rest of the day you are going to be aware of things that you see visually, for example, notice the color of the car in front of you when you drive, memorize the license plate, and what people are wearing. Be extremely visual in your day. But not only that, I would like you to work with your claircognizance, too. So start to "guess" which elevator is going to come first when you hit the button, "guess" the order of the person in front of you at the coffee shop, or "guess" what a colleague will bring to work for lunch.

When you start to combine your senses, they will become more and more heightened.

Stay present when you work this way, and continue this for the next twenty-four hours.

Don't forget to complete your automatic writing and dream journal.

If you would like to practice giving another reading, then this will certainly help you increase the strength of these senses.

Well done!

Day 42—Review Day

1. How have your senses developed this week with the exercises that have been given?

2. Do you feel that you are naturally clairvoyant or claircognizant? If so, please explain your reasons for this.

3. Did you enjoy the automatic writing? What did you discover?

4. Have you found that your dreams have become more vivid? Have you had any visitations?

5. Please re-read your fairytale. How does it resonate with you in your life right now? What did you discover, if anything about yourself?

WELCOME TO WEEK *Seven*

Last week we concentrated on the senses of sight and knowing, and this week we will look at our feeling and hearing. Defining the senses is something that a medium *has* to understand. When starting to work mediumistically, we question where the information comes from. We see things, then we hear something that is so random we shouldn't be hearing it, and then we feel something. In the beginning, when we are developing, we believe that a message is always going to come through the same way. And when it doesn't and it comes through another way, we are shocked. We question it and become confused and think "huh…I normally get my signs and information another way." But think about it—you are sitting in a garden drinking your favorite beverage; you absorb your surroundings using all of your senses.

- You *feel* the warmth of the sun on your body.
- You *smell* the scent of the flowers and the trees.
- You *see* the nature that is around you.
- You *hear* the rustle of the leaves and the birds in the trees.
- You *taste* the flavor of your drink.
- You *know* that the seat you are sitting on supports you.

Unless you have one or more of these senses disabled, then you will utilize all of them unconsciously. We take them for granted.

We get our information from Spirit using *all* of our senses, not just one of them. However, it's because we take them for granted that we suddenly become shocked because we "recognize" the sense consciously in a different way via a message from Spirit.

Day 43

We are going to focus on clairaudience for the next few days. This is the sense of hearing. This sense is something that has always been easy for me, and it's the one gift that I would not want to lose. I am constantly working on it to heighten and fine tune it. Even though I am partially deaf, it's the one sense that is developed. You will find that if you have a sense missing or partially missing, then this will be the psychic sense that is strongest. It is because you don't use the physical sense. Please don't get hung up on "seeing" Spirits as you can gain more information from "hearing" Spirits.

Today's Exercise

Start focusing on developing and noticing how you get information through your hearing. This can be through words that are placed in your mind, music that you start to sing, or words that you hear others speak. We get messages through various means.

Today you need to start to be aware of what you are hearing in your mind and also what you hear physically. You are going to spend twenty-four hours being aware of everything that just "comes" to you. That includes any songs that you get.

Use your journal to jot notes about what is given to you. Be aware of the sounds around your life and how you are accustomed to them. You may discover that your environment is actually quite noisy and you didn't realize it.

I remember one student did this exercise and ended up moving apartments because he didn't realize how noisy his surroundings were until he stopped and was aware.

Listen to everything, including the wind, since you may hear hidden messages in nature that are being given to you.

Day 44

You may struggle with clairaudience because it takes a great deal of *trust* to deliver a message that is solely based on listening to what you hear, and most of the time the information sounds like it is coming from yourself. You will doubt that it's coming from Spirit. It is only through practice and validation that you will finally gain the belief that you are correct with the message. There is no harm in being wrong or admitting that you are wrong. Someone who admits that they are wrong is someone who works without ego.

Surrendering to the message is important with clairaudience; you may not get the whole message, and it will just be words that will come to your head, as I mentioned yesterday. Random words will pop into your mind, and you won't know what it means. It takes a great deal of confidence to deliver that one word. Again, it reverts back to trust. When you fully trust the information that Spirit have, then they can deliver so much more.

There is an easy way for you to understand whether it's Spirit or your mind when you start to work.

All you need to do is talk to yourself.

Simple!

I know you are probably laughing and saying yeah, yeah, but seriously the more questions that you ask the more you answers you will get from Spirit.

Now, you have to listen carefully about how you get the information. This is the key. So when you ask a question, if you are given the answer as you finish off the sentence, then you are getting a genuine message of guidance. Your conscious mind is stepping in and thinking about the answer, as it only takes a split second for your conscious mind to start thinking.

Today's Exercise

Throughout the course of the day, ask Spirit to be with you, and start asking questions and notice how the questions are answered before you finish. Now you have to be aware that if you think about a topic and then you decide to ask a question, then your conscious mind has had time to process the answer, so that is not going to work.

Just ask random questions in your mind and see what comes forward.

Day 45

Those who develop clairaudience as their strongest sense are often musically minded; they can hear a piece of music and sing or play it immediately. You will find that they have very adept listening skills, too, because they listen to the information that they are getting from the Spirit that they are communicating with.

As a beginner music, sounds, and words will pop into your mind, and you may wonder what they are but you need to have the confidence to say what you get. This may have become easier for you since you have been working with your hearing for a few days now.

If you wish to work as a medium, you have to remember that if you hear something randomly, like a song, then it could be a song that shows a very special connection between the client and the Spirit. Withholding that piece of information, as small and as insignificant as it seems, could be a vital piece of information for the client.

Today's Exercise

Sitting in your sacred space, you will need to have access to a music library or playlists. It could be a CD or MP3 player that you will be able to use.

Sit quietly and ask for Spirit to connect with you. Remember to breathe and allow your mind to settle.

Put your CD player, MP3 player, or computer on shuffle, and notice the song that comes on and the words that are being sung. You will find hidden messages in the songs that come on.

Repeat this exercise as often as you need too. This is going to be a daily exercise for the remainder of the week.

Continue listening to everything that you get as you are out and about in your daily life. Never question anything that comes forward in your mind or the thoughts that you get. You may think that you are talking to yourself but you are not… it's Spirit connecting to you…. Just say thank you!

Day 46

Over the next two days we are going to embrace clairsentience, which is "clear feeling."

Everyone's strongest sense in the beginning is clairsentience. This is something that has developed naturally over the years. It's our survival mechanism. When we *felt* we were in danger, we took notice and got ourselves out of that situation. When we *felt* that someone wasn't being honest with us, we lost trust in that person. These are things that we do unconsciously in life. We react to situations because of how our bodies react. This is our clairsentience. You will find that some people will be naturally more clairsentient than others because they class themselves as "empaths."

Your heart is open, you are aware of how others feel, and you will react to it through your physical body.

When our bodies react—and when we have a "feeling" about something—we listen.

You may not notice that you are clairsentient because it's already so highly developed, and you take it for granted.

Let me explain that even though I have said that everyone has developed this sense, there will only be a few who will use it, and it's generally those who are in touch with their bodies and their own emotions.

We all have "gut reactions" that we don't listen to. Now it's time to sit up and take notice of them.

You may consider clairsentience to be "intuition." Well it *is* intuition, but there is also a significant difference since a Spirit will also "impress" emotions, pains, and feelings from their physical lives on readers, which might be ignored by mediums because they are so concerned with trying to *see* or *hear* Spirit.

It's so easy for a Spirit to work with clairsentience because of the connection that they will have through the auric field. The Spirit will connect with the etheric template of your aura, which will resonate with you on your physical level through the etheric aura.

Today's Exercise

Sit or stand in your sacred space, and imagine that you are pushing your aura out beyond the walls of the room. As you are imagining that your aura is going out, you can re-enforce it by pushing your hands out to the side. Always push your aura out to the side so that you can connect to Spirit.

As you are doing this, ask for Spirit to connect with your aura, and see if you can feel Spirit coming through and where they connect in your aura.

Record your experiences in your journal.

Try to continue to do this for the rest of the week, and enjoy connecting with Spirit.

Day 47

When you can connect and feel the Spirit in your aura, you will get remarkable results as long as you say what you are getting and don't fear being wrong. This fear of being wrong can introduce self-doubt, no matter how experienced you are. There are days when I get into my head, can't focus, and then start to worry that everything I am getting is wrong. Reality is it isn't wrong; it's just that my mind thinks it is.

However, clairsentience can really help in this situation. I watch how my body reacts when I say a piece of information, and when it's incorrect it will feel as though I have been hit in the stomach, and then I say, "I'm sorry, that doesn't 'feel' right." Or there are times that I can be so spot-on that I get tingles up my thighs.

The same will happen to you. Your body will react in different ways. It won't be the same as me, but you will find your own way of working. It's like a signal to say you are right or wrong.

Your body may not react when you are correct, but I can guarantee when you say something that is off, your body will feel off. If that is the case, say it.

For example, there is nothing wrong is saying this:

"I believe that I have your father in Spirit with me and that he passed with cancer.... Hmmm, I'm sorry that doesn't feel right, one moment.... No, I believe I was wrong. I actually feel it was your mother who passed with cancer. Would I be correct in saying that?"

It shows credibility and honesty. Mediums who work with confidence will always shine because they *believe* in their messages!

So when the body reacts it's because the clairsentience is kicking in, and you have to sit up and take note.

Today's Exercise

You are going to feel your body; you are going to really feel your every move. So for the next twenty-four hours I would like you to be very aware and mindful of the movements your body makes, whether it's fast or slow, and how you react to situations and places. When you say something that isn't correct in your everyday life, watch how your body reacts. It will "feel" wrong.

Another way of connecting with your body is through music and dance. You are going to put on some music and dance around. Put on your favorite music, and move your body to the music, not worrying about who is watching you.

Be aware of how your body moves and what it feels like to be free.

Have lots of fun today. Tomorrow you will be doing a reading, so be prepared to ask a friend.

Day 48

Now that you have worked with your clairaudience and clairsentience, you are now going to give a reading to someone and work mainly through these senses.

Today's Exercise

Ask a friend or someone who is willing to help you to sit in front of you and relax. You can either ask who your friend wishes to connect with or it can just be free flowing and allow the Spirit to come to you. If you have never done this work before, I would suggest asking who your friend wishes to connect with but only getting the name and relationship. If you have done Mediumship before then try to be free with the information.

Sit directly in front of your friend, and push your aura out to the side and ask for Spirit to come and connect with you. Say everything that you are getting. Don't forget to ask your "client" for validation throughout.

Have lots of fun and enjoy the experience.

Day 49—Review Day

1. Were you able to distinguish the difference between your own mind and Spirit when listening for information? Please explain your answer.

2. What were some of the songs on your playlist that had hidden messages? Please explain what those messages were for you.

3. Did you notice when Spirit was connecting with your aura? What did you notice about how your body reacted?

4. Did you enjoy feeling your body and dancing around in the house?

5. What did you notice about your senses this week? Do you feel that they are getting stronger in a Mediumistic way?

6. Now that you have given a reading, what are your thoughts about giving readings? Please explain how you felt about this and if you are encountering any issues.

WELCOME TO WEEK *Eight*

Congratulations! You are in the final week, you have made it this far, and you have probably had some incredible life-changing experiences. Everyone is going to have a different experience, and this is *your* experience and no one else's. You have to embrace what you have been through and realize that you will develop in your own time. Not everyone is supposed to be a medium, but you will discover that you *can* connect with your loved ones and you probably have throughout the duration of this work.

Getting to this stage has taken dedication and commitment from yourself, and you have had time to reflect on your life and journey with Spirit. You have achieved great results, and you should be extremely proud of yourself. Over the last few weeks, you have focused on working on individual senses, and they will continue to develop the more you work with them. It's been an incredible journey that you have been on, and you can guarantee that Spirit *will* work with you when you need them.

You will need to find people to read for this week, so please ask your friends, family, and work colleagues if you can practice with them.

Day 50

You have now isolated four of your major senses; you will find, however, that your senses of smell and taste will develop the more you work with them. These are known as clairalience, which is "clear smelling," and clairgustance, which means "clear tasting." These happen quite often when Spirit are trying to impress upon me what they really liked to eat or smell. Now, you will find that these two senses work together; this is because when you smell a certain food, your taste buds are stimulated. While these are individual senses, there is an intimate relationship between the two of them. We will isolate these senses so that you have an understanding, however, do not worry if you do not get information from Spirit this way. It's just another way to enhance the experience with Spirit that you already have.

Smell is often associated with memory. Let me explain a little. The olfactory bulb is the most forward part of the brain, which is associated to the perception of odors. It is also the part of the brain that is associated with memories and feelings. So when we smell something, it can bring in a flood of memories. For example, I grew up with my mother smoking, and every morning she would have a cup of tea, a slice of toast, and a cigarette while she was putting on her makeup for work using a little handheld mirror on the sofa.

My mother quit smoking when I was in my late teenage years, and I never thought about that image of my mother ever again because it wasn't something that I saw because when she stopped smoking she had to change her whole morning routine so that she wasn't tempted. Years later I had a friend stay over at my house who smoked, and in the morning, like a good hostess, I asked her what she would like for breakfast before she left, and she said a slice of toast and a cup of tea. I made this, she went outside for a cigarette before leaving, and as she was coming in to hug me good-bye after, I smelled my mom. A mixture of toast, butter, tea with sugar, and nicotine...it suddenly flashed me back to the image that I had grown up with as a child.

Recently in a reading, I saw that exact image again, and the smell of cigarettes came to me, and so I could tell the woman what her husband had every morning: a slice of toast, cup of tea, and a cigarette.

So as you can see that certain smells will flash you back to times that you remember, and Spirit will use the memories that you have in your conscious brain to trigger things about themselves so that you can deliver the message. It's quite incredible when you think about it.

The same thing happens with taste. As babies, we had more taste buds and if you notice, *everything* goes in babies' mouths. We came to like certain tastes and textures, and as we grew up the number of taste buds decreased, causing our sense of taste becomes weaker. When we chew food, we force air through our nasal passages, which carries the smell of food with it. Without the interconnection of taste and smell, we would not be able to grasp complex flavors. We also have associations to food that we liked and didn't like as children.

When we get tastes coming through, Spirit impresses their likes and dislikes on us. Taste is a chemical sense and is like smelling. There are five basic kinds of taste: sweet, sour, bitter, salty, and savory, so we often get impressions of these tastes given to us. We can say to the person we are working with that "I am tasting chocolate, which I believe means your loved one had a sweet tooth?" and often you will find that the answer is yes!

Today's Exercise

As you are going about your day, notice the smells and the tastes that you encounter, and see if any take you back to a period of time in your life. Be extremely present as you do this. The more experiences that you have in your consciousness, the more Spirit will be able to pull on those experiences, and it will be easier for them to deliver the messages to you.

Day 51

All of the senses have now been isolated, and you have started to realize that each sense works hand in hand. Yesterday as you were going about your day working with both taste and smell, you were also working with your other senses and creating a whole experience.

For example, you might have walked past a hot dog stand and stopped to smell the hot dogs, which instantly made your mouth water as the scent activated the taste buds, as food needs liquid to create the actual sensation of taste. While this was happening, you were looking at the stand, hearing the sizzling of the meat on the grill and the busyness of the surrounding areas, and feeling the heat that was coming from the grill.

All of your senses work together in daily life, and the same will happen when you work as a medium. When Spirit are trying to show you some evidential facts of their lives so that you can share them, you will not just get the information through one sense. You will get it through *all* of your senses. The more you surrender to Spirit, the more your senses will be alive and you will allow yourself to let go and experience the whole reading through the perception of the Spirit. This is a remarkable experience when it happens, and it's only fear that holds us back.

When Spirit connect they will be connecting in a way that you will understand, so they will work with the senses that are the strongest. Clairaudience is my strongest sense, but if I don't quite catch what was given to me, I will ask for it to be given to me in a different way. The key is to *ask* for the information, and just because you asked doesn't mean that you will hear the answer. You could receive a vision instead.

Let me give you an example. When I give a reading, I will get so many things at once, and I have to remember them as I continue to talk about what I have received. So as I talk, I'm always playing catch up. Take a look at the diagram on the following page, and you will understand what happens when I give a reading.

As you can see, as a medium you have to give what you get and not change anything. The secret is to continue talking; don't sit there with your eyes closed, panicking and willing the Spirit to come and chat. Just open your eyes and talk to the person opposite you. About anything. You will find that as you talk the receiver will be able to connect with your story whether you realize it or not. So just say what you get.

...

Time Line of Communication

Spirit Communication	Medium's Communication
Hearing I used to like shopping **Seeing** Looking at the foods and colors **Feeling** Excited and fun **Knowing** Know that this is one of their favorite past times and that the client used to go shopping with them **Taste / Smell** Coffee smell and Ice Cream	Your mother is talking about it being your birthday and that she never forgot your birthday. I am seeing that she would always bake you a cake on your birthday. Actually, she is taking me back to a time when you were a child and you had M&Ms on the top of your cake and, at the birthday party, you kept stealing the M&Ms off the top of the cake, and when it came to lighting the candles and singing happy birthday, there were none left because you had eaten them all. She was indicating that the red M&Ms are your favourite.
Hearing She was my only daughter, but she has a son that I was very close to. **Seeing** Seeing an image of the boy with brown hair and blue eyes. **Feeling** A great deal of love **Knowing** I know that mother spent a lot of time with the boy, and that she felt guilty that she didn't get to say goodbye to him.	Your mother is telling me that she loved to go shopping and it was one of her favorite past times. She is feeling excited about when she would go shopping, but I am not seeing clothes. I am seeing food, which would make me believe that she loved food and cooking. I believe that you and she would go shopping all the time and that it was a like a kind of outing for you, as she is making me aware of Coffee and Ice Cream. I feel as though you would get one of these things when you shopped together.
	Your mother is making me aware that you are her only daughter and that you have a son. She is showing me that your son has dark hair and blue eyes and that she adores him and was extremely close to him. I do believe that she never got the chance to say goodbye to him and that she was sad about that as they spent a lot of time together.

same time → *message* → *same time* → *message*

Today's Exercise

Be very present in your daily life, and notice how all your senses work together.

Once you have spent some time being present, give someone a reading. If you need to ask who the person wishes to connect with, then that is fine, as long as they only give you the relationship and the name. Use all of your senses to deliver the message in the way that you get it. You will find that it will flow. Just relax, and do not worry. The only person who puts pressure on you is you. Even if you just get a few hits, practice makes perfect. What you have to remember is that the mediums that you have seen working on TV or in audience readings have probably been doing this for years, and they were once in the same position as you.

Day 52

Now that you have had some experience in giving a message, and you have practiced a few times, it's important for you to know about the stages of a reading and understand how to deliver the message.

It's time now to break down the communication and deliver the message.

Within a reading there are three different phases of communication. I always associate it with a workout. You have to warm up then, once you are ready, you can then do the bulk of your exercise, and then once you have done that, you need to cool down and stretch.

It's the same with communication with Spirit.

As you know, when you are dealing with Spirit, you are dealing with personalities, and those personalities may be shy, wary, or quiet. On the other hand they can also be loud, bubbly, and brash. But ultimately treat them with respect and encourage them to talk to you.

You have to allow them to build up their trust in you. Put yourself in their shoes: would you want to tell all your secrets to a stranger?

It's also important for you to put your clients at ease. If they are not comfortable, their Spirit will not be happy talking to them through you.

Remember to use all your senses to gather information. You will be doing exercises this week that will help in developing your senses and working with phases of communication.

Phase One

This first phase occurs when you begin the message. You will feel the energy change around you, especially on one side of your body. It's rare that you will feel it on both sides and, if you do, there is often a reason, such as the body hasn't crossed but the Spirit has (such as for those who are in comas).

You will feel that Spirit has drawn close to you. The information that Spirit gives you may not be clear, as the link is not strong yet. Here your job is to identify whom you are talking to. They will do this by providing information about themselves from when they were on the earth plane. Things to look for:

- Male or female?
- What caused their passing?
- How long they have been gone?
- The relationship to the client.

Ask them questions to let them know you are interested.

If you are struggling here, ask your Spirit Guides to help, and ask them also to raise your vibrations. However, remember you are dealing with a Spirit person, and you have to build up their trust. The more information you share that they have given you, the stronger the link will be.

Phase Two

This middle phase occurs when Spirit holds a strong link. Here is the opportunity to give some information of events that have happened since they died. We call this "knowledge of recent events" and it gives us proof of ongoing existence.

This is the period in which the real substance of the message is given. This is the time to ask the questions that you wish to ask. The information comes through quickly and clearly here. When the essence of the message is given and the communicator feels satisfied, the Spirit will then begin the withdrawal process. Things that may be discussed with you:

Spirit may tell you about events they witnessed while in Spirit that has recently happened to the client.

Answer the questions that clients need answering.

Spirit may tell you more information about themselves.

You may also take on the mannerisms of Spirit from when they were on the earth plane.

Other questions that you may wish to ask them:
- What relationship did you and the client have?
- What was the cause of death?
- How long since you passed over?
- Who greeted you on the other side?
- How are you now?
- Who do you need to get a message to?

- What is the message? (Remember it can be so simple that we may even miss it, such as "Happy Birthday," "I Love You," "I'm OK," or "I'm with mom!")

You will come up with your own additional questions.

Problems can arise in Phase Two if you don't work hard at establishing a strong enough link with Spirit during the first phase of the message. You will find that the communication with Spirit will close quickly.

Phase Three

This final phase occurs while when Spirit is stepping away from you. The information begins to become foggier and a little less clear as the energy between you as the medium and the Spirit starts to separate.

This is when you need to close the message and thank the Spirit for the information that you have received. When I know this is happening I ask clients if they have any other questions since I want to try and answer their questions while I am still holding the link. Sometimes Spirit come back strong again, sometimes they don't. Don't be disappointed if you don't get all the questions answered. As I have said before, Spirit tell you what you need to know.

Also *please* do not allow your client to "test" you in any way. If your client says, "If it is my mom, she would tell you the name of her favorite song," then tell the client honestly that you never received that information.

Don't guess.

Trivial things like song titles are irrelevant to Spirit. If you have given enough evidence about that Spirit, then Spirit will be satisfied. This happens many times when clients expect names to come through. Names come through sometimes, but not all the time. You may be listening or looking out for something else and miss the name. If Spirit feel it's important to give a name, then they will make sure you hear it or show you someone you know with the same name.

Think of the film *Ghost*. Sam (Patrick Swayze) wanted the medium's attention so he pestered her…the same would happen to you. If you have not gotten all the important information across, they will not leave you. To them their earth name may not be important.

It is at this point that many mediums encounter difficulty and may sit in complete silence or give up and conclude the message without offering any tangible evidence or information. This can be very frustrating because the medium didn't give Spirit the opportunity to get close enough to get a strong message across.

If this happens, ask for help from your guides, and ask them to raise your vibrations high enough to get the messages that Spirit need to deliver. Don't ever worry about going back to Phase One and reconnecting and getting more evidential facts that will build up the connection again. You will find that if several Spirits come through, you can go in and out of Phase One and Two constantly throughout the reading.

As a medium you must understand that the first stage of a message may not be very clear. Spirit are still feeling their way around and trying to blend with your energy field. At this stage, you must work hard, maintain some form of verbal interaction, and attempt to strengthen the link so that you and Spirit can pass on to the next stage of the communication. Be brave and give whatever information you get, so that the communicator will be given the opportunity to draw closer and work with you even more strongly.

This requires that you work hard and not give up!

Spirit will only give you the information that clients *need* to know, so if they don't need to know about an illness or a death then they will not tell you. However, if they do need to warn your clients about something, then they will let you know. It is then your job to pass the message across as you see fit, using the words that you feel are right.

It is always better to ask clients at the start of any reading if they want to know everything!

Today's Exercise

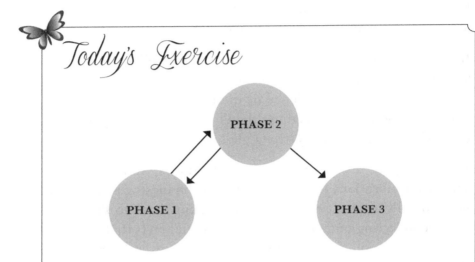

Again you are going to give a reading but try to work within the Phases of Communication. Naturally Phase One and Two will weave in and out of each other, but don't worry, just have a go at delivering the message. Also make sure that you record the reading on your phone or computer.

You are recording it for your purposes only, you *must* let your client know that they are being recorded. If you choose to give a copy to the person that you are reading for, then that is up to you, but *please* ensure that they know that you are learning.

Never give a prediction about future situations unless you feel confident. You are working mediumistically, and therefore you're only trying to connect with Spirit. If Spirit gives you information about your client's life, then please state that you are getting it from Spirit. You are working toward Mediumship, not being a psychic. As I have explained before, there is a very big difference.

Once you have given your reading, listen back to it and hear how you deliver your message and what you say. Most people, including myself, do not like this exercise because they see their flaws, but it's the best way to learn and grow. Think about how you could change the delivery of the reading, what things you could change, and how it may come across.

Please do not get disheartened…you have come this far, and all you are going to do is grow from this experience.

Relax and make sure that you have fun and laugh because Spirit's energy is raised through fun and laughter.

Good luck!

Day 53

We are going to continue our days of readings. The more that you do, the better you will become. It's like anything new that you are learning: you have to practice. If you don't feel that you are connecting, continue to practice. You *will* get there. You may also surprise yourself with how much information you do get, which can be eye-opening.

Today's Exercise

Now that you have given two readings in the last few days, it's time to reflect and think about how you could change your readings and what you could do differently. With this in mind, you are going to give another reading. This reading doesn't have to be long, but you need to put into practice the information that you have learned.

Here are some things to think about:

- Remember your last reading, and think about how you can change the delivery of the message.
- What would you have said differently?
- Use *all* your senses.
- Remember to work with the Phases of Communication.
- Say what you get.
- Remember to ask questions of Spirit and relay the answers will come in a way that you understand.

Day 54

It's important when you think about being a medium that you understand the dos and don'ts of Mediumship. There is a huge responsibility because the client is in your hands. You could open wounds and situations that the client is not prepared to deal with. So when you are going through this book, please let your friends know that you are practicing.

Ask them not to test you throughout this process.

Let's look at the dos and don'ts of being a medium.

- Don't put pressure on yourself; if you do not connect, then don't worry.

- Don't ask leading questions. The only questions that you should ask are if the client can relate to what you are saying or, if you are struggling to get information, ask who the client would like to connect with. That is all you need to start you off.

- Don't read for someone who has had a loved one pass within the last three months (this isn't always possible, but try to be aware of this).

- Don't allow your client to test you.

- Don't read someone without permission

- Do choose your words carefully.

- Do be sensitive to the situation.

- Do listen to your clients if they want to talk.

- Do read for your client in the same way that you would want to be read for.

- Do ask your clients if they wish to know everything.

- Do make your clients feel comfortable.

- Do make sure you give them time to ask questions.

- Do relax and be at ease.

- Do have fun.

These are the essential elements of giving a reading, but you must be authentic and have integrity.

People often ask me what they should look for when they go see a medium, so I have compiled a list to help you source the right medium for you.

- Try to get a recommendation or find someone with a strong reputation. I recommend many certified mediums in my directory who have all gone through a testing process and have passed to a high standard.

- Just because someone is recommended, doesn't mean that medium is right for you. Always go with your gut feeling about whether it is the right fit for you.
- Remember that you may have to wait for your reading; you may not be able to get in next day with a good medium.
- Did you feel comfortable with the communication that you had while booking the reading?
- Do not give any information to the medium before the reading except for your name and telephone number. The medium should not need any more information.
- Prepare for your reading by asking your loved ones to come through.
- Prepare a list of questions that you may need answered by Spirit.
- Do not expect too much. When we have expectations, we are disappointed. Just enjoy the experience.
- Do not test mediums; be open to the information that they give you.
- Think outside the box, and know that Spirit will deliver the message however they can to the medium. You may not get the person that you want at first but stay and listen.
- Remember that we forget things, so do not disregard things as you may find that you will walk away and remember nothing. It's called psychic amnesia.
- Ask questions if you need more information.
- Relax and enjoy the experience.

Today's Exercise

Think about what you would like to get out of a reading and also if you would like to work as a medium. Think about your strong points and what you can offer your clients. Make time for yourself in your sacred space, and consider your journey through this book and what you think your next step is. Would you like to pursue this, or do you wish to just use these exercises to connect with your own loved ones.

There is no pressure and no expectation on you. If you don't know the way forward, then that is **OK**; it will come to you in time.

Take some time to reflect on your journey so far.

Day 55

Do you want to be a medium? Not everyone believes in Mediumship so you have to be prepared to have people judge you, and sadly you will grow a thick skin, but you can still remain compassionate and loving toward everyone that you meet. There is a fine line. Having said that, you also need a life. You have to ensure that you have other interests so that you can escape the Spirit when you need to.

The other thing you have to ensure is that you stay grounded and real. You can't afford to have an ego; it will put people off.

Mediumship can help many people in life. Just knowing that life continues is essential to people so that they can have a belief in something.

Let's look at the reasons why Mediumship can benefit people's lives.

- People facing death want to know that they are going to see their loved ones when they pass.
- People losing loved ones want to know that their souls are still alive and they are still watching over them.
- We seek guidance from Spirit, believing that they have the knowledge that we need in life.
- We need something to believe in.
- We connect with guides and angels so that we can be given divine guidance beyond our own higher self.

And the list goes on….

Mediumship to me is vital in everyone's life; it can help people grieve, overcome situations, believe in themselves, believe in others, and it can help them connect with their souls and access vital information that they all need that will help them.

Being a medium doesn't come without its ups and downs, but ultimately it's an incredible gift. Life as a medium can be extremely rewarding, but it comes with expectations and responsibilities. People do put expectations on you and want so much from you, but it's only natural when you have clients who need to have that connection to carry on with their lives. You have to take responsibility for your gift and know that you have to work with integrity and authenticity.

When you fully surrender to Spirit, you will understand that you have to be committed to the work, because your life will never be the same. You will change as a person, you will face lessons for yourself through other people's readings, and you will be tested. Having said this, being a medium is one of the most rewarding experiences that you can ever have. You will see love and healing merge together in the moment when you connect to Spirit. Your connection really can be life changing.

Today's Exercise

It's a time of reflection. Think back over reading the book and how you have changed and what you have understood and learned as a person and as a medium.

Meditate and connect with Spirit through writing, allowing the connection to flow. You will find that you will get guidance from Spirit.

Congratulations on completing eight weeks of dedicating your life to Spirit. By allowing yourself to fully surrender to Spirit, you can believe that it will change your life in so many ways. You will see the world through a whole new set of eyes.

I will leave you with a Message from Spirit that is given to the advanced mediums as they begin their journey.

Message from Spirit

When you work with us, you are working with yourself, your highest good, and also for the grace of God and Spirit.

It should be considered an honor for a medium to work with Spirit, as you are being given the opportunity to do the work that you have been put on this earth to do.

Sadly everyone's world has become overtaken and consumed by life.

This is a special time in your existence. Minds are coming together for a reason and to spread the messages that we have. It's ironic since a world like yours that needs so much healing has forgotten what is real.

It's those that are among you who are opening themselves up to the world that we live in and the world that you have come from who are educating those who have forgotten their way.

It's not an easy task, but it's a task that you have agreed to take on, and we will help you with it but we will not always be able to guide.

Your ego lets you down along the way. I know that you are saying it won't, but rest assured that we know it will happen, but we promise that we will never let you down or walk away from you. When these times are encountered we will stand with you until you come back to the nest again.

Only when you are ready will you return to your pathway. You may stay on it for a while but you may also take a break. But you must always return; you have been chosen, and you have decided that your pathway is to serve.

We will serve you well if you serve us. Many extraordinary things may happen to you while you're working with us and for us. That is because we are rewarding you for your service. You will be rewarded materialistically, but is this something that you want or desire…of course, because you need it. Is fame and fortune what you want?

If it is, you are in the wrong line, and we cannot do this for you…. We will certainly help but the doors will only open if it's something that you are meant to do and teach others. It's your ego, so let go of it.

Open your eyes and start to live your life with the realization that your destiny is within you and that you're on the right pathway.

Yes, your life may have been tough and difficult, but that is for a reason. You have been guided to take this road of hardship so that you can journey with other souls and help them through life.

Do you think that we enjoy watching you suffer without us? No we don't, but we will always guide you well and help you take each step through your journey. Some steps may be harder than others, but through this work you will find the courage to open your eyes and learn that you are fulfilling your destiny and dream. Know that you are always loved and no one is going to judge you....

Those who judge you do not understand nor do they understand life; they do not live life to its fullest. We cannot change those people, but they are put in your pathway to test you, and you can survive those tests because you will always come out smiling.

You won't win because it's not a game and, if you think about it that way, your ego will come alive again, and this is something that you can ill afford. You have to rise above it and enjoy the challenge.

May your hearts always be open, a smile be on your face, and your arms outstretched for the embrace that is so needed for others to heal. We wish you well on your journey through Spirit.

Day 56—Review Day

1. Think about your last two senses and the exercise where you were mindful of your senses. Did they spark any memories for you?

2. Do you feel that you are connecting to Spirit stronger than before?

3. How did you feel with your first reading when you consciously brought all your senses together?

4. When you listened to the recording of your reading, what did you feel you could have done differently?

5. Did you find that your next reading was better once you had analyzed your reading?

6. Please write about how your journey with this book has impacted your life. What do you hope to do with your Mediumship from this point on?

Congratulations in unleashing the medium within you!.

You may have loved this journey or found it incredibly hard, whatever your experience, just know that Mediumship takes time and practice, and once you have started then you have to continue to practice every single day.

Even though I have been doing readings for many years I still continue to practice by doing daily exercises and working with clients. Mediumship is like a muscle, the more you train it the stronger it becomes.

You have gotten this far, you have dedicated yourself to Spirit, and now is the time to grow and continue to learn from Spirit or other courses and books. You have done so well.

I will share with you one thing... I could not image a day without Spirit in my life. I am never alone, I always have someone to bounce my ideas off and Spirit will laugh at my jokes when no one else will.

When you can surrender to the infinite possibilities that Spirit can show you, your life will never be the same again.

I wish you well on your journey with Spirit.

With Love

Lisa xoxo

Answers to Exercise—Day 5

1. The person's name is Victor John Williams—known as Jack Williams.

2. He is my paternal grandfather.

3. He was a total jokester—very funny—but he also had a serious side. Very friendly and sociable. He was the life and soul of the party.

4. He hated lateness. He loved children, music, and he had a thing about his shoes and coats—they always had to be of a good quality. He loved horse racing, playing cards, singing, soccer, and golf. He also collected stamps and coins.

5. He has one child and two grandchildren.

6. The sex of the child is male. He has one granddaughter and one grandson.

7. He went to the hospital with a chest infection and died three days later of an embolism in the stomach. It was a very sudden passing.

8. He worked as an engineer, but he was an all-around handy man who was able to fix a car or paint a house. He was in the army in his younger days.

9. We were both singers, and we often sang together. Another memory is lots of vacations we spent together at the "caravan" in Brean Sands in the United Kingdom. He adored my son, Charlie, so he may also give you memories of Charlie.

10. His nationality is English.

BIBILOGRAPHY

Kardec, Allan. *The Spirits' Book*. Spastic Cat Press, 2012.

Kübler-Ross, Elisabeth, & Kessler, David. *On Grief and Grieving: Finding the Meaning of Grief Through the Five Stages of Loss.* Scribner, 2007.

Virtue, Doreen. *Angel Numbers 101: The Meaning of 111, 123, 444 and Other Number Sequences.* Hay House, 2008.

NIV Holy Bible, Zondervan, 2012.

Stokes, Doris. *A Host of Voices: The Second Doris Stokes Collection.* Little, Brown Book Group, 2000.

ABOUT THE AUTHOR

Lisa Williams is a world-renowned medium and clairvoyant with an amazing ability to communicate with those who have passed on to the other side.

Born in England, Lisa was discovered by Merv Griffin and introduced to audiences through two seasons of her own hit show, *Lisa Williams: Life Among the Dead*, along with *Voices from the Other Side* and *Lisa Williams Live*. All of these shows are now airing around the world. She has also appeared on *Keeping Up with The Kardashians*, *Anderson Cooper*, *Oprah*, *The Ricki Lake Show*, *Good Morning America*, *The Today Show*, *Larry King Live* and *Jimmy Kimmel Live*.

When she's not performing in front of large live audiences worldwide, Lisa offers workshops and courses in mediumship, developing psychic ability, intuition and meditation. In 2013 she launched the Lisa Williams International School of Spiritual Development (lwissd.com), through which she delivers her classes with her own unique and very hands-on method of teaching. Through the school, Lisa offers access to her personally trained and certified mediums and psychics who are part of the LWISSD Directory.

As well as workshops, Lisa offers a variety of online courses, from beginner to advanced levels. Her online video series, 'The Confident Soul', is aimed at building confidence within relationships and in the workplace. She is also the accomplished author of several books on mediumship and spirituality, including *Survival of the Soul* and *Life Among the Dead, I Speak to Dead People, Can You?* (retitled and republished in 2016 as *Was that a Sign from Heaven? How to Connect with the Afterlife*), and the insightful *Intuitive Soul Oracle Cards* designed to open our intuitive gifts and develop the psychic senses, and she is currently working on a comprehensive A-Z reference guide about the afterlife and a book that explores the topic of soul mates and soul connections. You can find more details on Lisa's work and events on her website, www. lisawilliams.com.

Lisa lives in New York State with her son, Charlie, and their two dogs, Max and Lucy.

Notes

Notes

Notes

Notes

Notes